A SHORT HISTORY OF NEWFOUNDLAND AND LABRADOR

Newfoundland Historical Society

2008

BOULDER
PUBLICATIONS

Library and Archives Canada Cataloguing in Publication

A Short History of Newfoundland and Labrador / Newfoundland
Historical Society.

Includes bibliographical references.
ISBN 978-0-9783381-8-3

1. Newfoundland and Labrador--History. I. Newfoundland Historical Society

FC2161.S48 2008   971.8   C2008-906261-2

© 2008 Newfoundland Historical Society

Newfoundland
Labrador

We acknowledge the financial support of the Government
of Newfoundland and Labrador through the Department of
Tourism, Culture and Recreation for our publishing program.

Published by
BOULDER PUBLICATIONS
11 Boulder Lane
Portugal Cove-St. Philip's, NL
A1M 2K1

Cover background photo by Dennis Flynn
Cover design and layout by Vanessa Stockley, Granite Studios

Printed in Canada

CONTENTS

The Newfoundland Historical Society thanks the authors for contributing their time and expertise to this book. We gratefully acknowledge a financial contribution from the Johnson Family Foundation toward the publication of this book. The Society and the authors also thank Jerry Bannister for his helpful comments and Toby Simpson for creating the maps. The Society and authors also express their appreciation to the Managing Editor Shannon Lewis-Simpson.

PREFACE

Jeff A. Webb

The first written history of Newfoundland was published by Chief Justice John Reeves in 1793, and during the next century it was followed by several accounts of the country's development, culminating in the monumental history of Judge D.W. Prowse in 1895.

The twentieth century saw few attempts to write a comprehensive history, in large measure because historians were not satisfied with an account that did not include the experiences of working people, native people, women, and other groups. Professional historians of the twentieth century re-evaluated Newfoundland and Labrador's political and economic development through intensive research. In the last quarter-century social historians, in particular, have addressed many gaps in our knowledge of average people's experiences. These scholars have given us a more complete and sophisticated knowledge of new topics and have re-assessed some of the sweeping generalizations about the past. Historians and archaeologists now see many factors that contributed to the extinction of the Beothuk, for example. Others have shown that our notions of the prohibition on European settlement were exaggerated and that the pattern of settlement reflected the nature of the fishery and the land itself. While fish merchants are villains in popular memory, the nature of the truck system was more varied and complex than we once believed. A few people who were unhappy with the outcome of the confederation debate of the 1940s wondered if a conspiracy had been in operation, but we now have a more complete and nuanced understanding of British and Canadian policy. Because this scholarship was largely published in specialized academic journals and books, it did not have the effect upon public knowledge of the past that the work merited. So the gap between the widespread beliefs about our past and scholarly opinion became progressively wider. That has been a matter of concern to the Newfoundland Historical Society.

The mission of the Newfoundland Historical Society is to bring knowledge and appreciation of the history of Newfoundland and Labrador to the public, which it fulfills through publications, lectures, and symposia. The NHS decided that the time was ripe for a slender volume which brought the views of some of the province's scholars to a wider public. Each contributor to this book was given strict limits as to chapter length, so difficult choices had to be made to leave out many fascinating and important details. The authors were given freedom to make a statement about aspects of our past that they feel are essential knowledge. Particular emphasis was given to the many areas in which popular notions are undermined by current research.

Each author has varied in his or her usage of the name of this place as the topic requires. The province of Newfoundland and Labrador is a recent usage and is not always appropriate when discussing earlier times. The coast of Labrador was assigned to Newfoundland only in 1763, and many times it is appropriate to speak of the two territories separately. Similarly, during some parts of our history we were a fishing station, a colony, a Dominion, and a province. To impose one word on all time periods would not be accurate. In this brief survey we also discuss many developments and aspects of people's lives which were common to people who lived in all the regions of what is now the Province of Newfoundland and Labrador.

This is not a complete history of Newfoundland and Labrador; such a thing would be impossible given the wealth of research that has already been done and the large number of topics which remain to be explored. Readers who find that this volume whets their appetite for greater knowledge of the themes explored here will find a list of suggested readings at the back of this volume which can be a starting place for an exploration of the varied and remarkable history of this place.

CHAPTER I

Native Peoples from the Ice Age to the Extinction of the Beothuk (c. 9,000 Years Ago to AD 1829)

Lisa Rankin

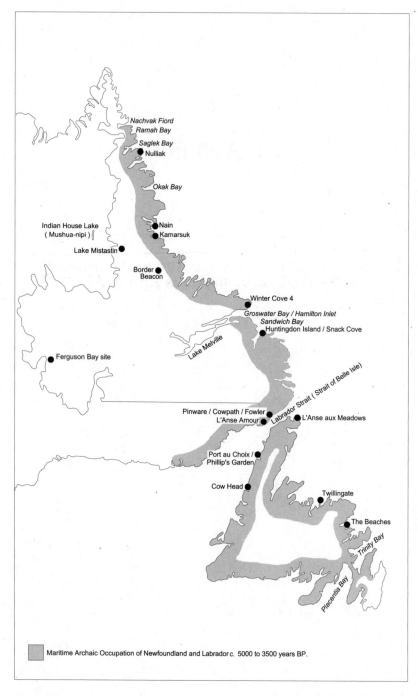

Key archaeological sites in Newfoundland and Labrador.

Newfoundland and Labrador was discovered by bands of explorers who left their known world to travel to lands they knew nothing about and could only hope would bring them prosperity. Once here, they stayed and settled, making use of the available abundant natural resources, but life was not always easy. The extreme climate and occasional fluctuations in resource availability meant that there were constant challenges, which sometimes resulted in tragedy.

The Labrador Archaic Pioneers

The first population to venture to this province arrived in Labrador between 8,000 and 9,000 years ago. These early explorers were AmerIndian hunters. Their distant ancestors had followed large game animals across the Bering land bridge connecting Siberia and Alaska during the last ice age. Once in North America they tracked and hunted mastodon and other large game animals to the south and east until they had explored much of the ice-free Americas. As the ice age drew to a close, the climate warmed, and the North American ecosystem changed. The large game animals that had thrived on the tundra-steppe and grasslands of the ice-age Americas were restricted to smaller territories. Many animals, such as the mastodon, became extinct. In order to survive, the early hunters had to adapt to these new environmental conditions by spending more time collecting plants and marine resources, but in some pockets of the New World, like the far northeast, hunting large game continued to be the primary focus. The glaciers that covered most of Labrador retreated from the shoreline in a northwesterly direction, allowing for ice-free zones on the southern coast of Labrador by 10,000 years ago, but this process took longer in other areas. For example, the central coast of Labrador was not free of glacial ice until 9,000 years ago. When the ice had gone, the slow process of re-vegetation began. The first plants to populate the barren lands were lichens, then small shrubs such as alder. Once established, these plants were able to provide basic fodder for herds of caribou that were quick to colonize the newly available land. The hunters were not far behind.

Stone artifacts from the Cowpath site, Labrador Straits: two knife blades (left) and three spear points (right) (photo: J. Tuck).

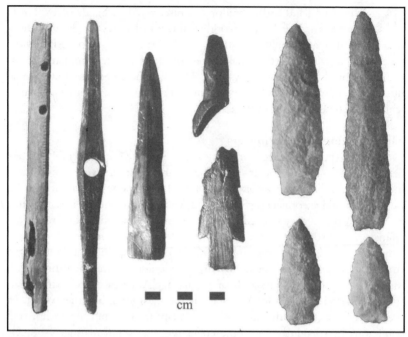

Artifacts from the L'Anse Amour burial site. Left to right: bone whistle, harpoon line handle (bone), socketed bone spear, bone harpoon head (upper), stemmed bone spear point (lower), four stone spear points (photo: J. Tuck).

The first evidence of these pioneers comes from the archaeological sites of Pinware Hill and Cowpath, which were located on the ancient beaches of the Labrador Straits between 8,300 and 9,000 years ago. These two small sites only hint at what life was like for these early settlers. They include evidence of chipped stone tools such as triangular projectile points used for hunting and thumbnail scrapers used to prepare animal hides. Because of the acidic soils no organic materials such as animal bone or plants were preserved at these sites and we cannot be certain about other aspects of their life; the projectile points, however, are similar to those used in other regions for hunting large game. The tools that were recovered from these sites bear a likeness to those recovered from archaeological contexts in the Maritimes. This similarity suggests that the first people to come to Labrador had originally inhabited the Maritimes. How they travelled from the Maritimes to Labrador is still poorly understood, but at some time they must have crossed the Gulf of St. Lawrence to the lower north shore of Québec and then on to Labrador. To undertake such a journey these early hunters probably had to travel with the aid of some kind of watercraft. Given that both the Pinware Hill and Cowpath sites were situated on beach fronts, these early hunters may well have had other knowledge about the marine environment and the ability to harvest such marine resources as seals and other sea mammals. Whatever the situation, they certainly adapted well to the coastal Labrador environment over the ensuing centuries.

Within a thousand years of the human discovery of Labrador, people had settled the Straits region and had adapted their way of life to coincide with the local ecosystem. Archaeologists now refer to these settlers as the Labrador Archaic Indians. While caribou hunting was still an important part of their economic activity, we have direct evidence that these early settlers were making significant use of the abundant coastal resources in the region. One of the most exciting archaeological discoveries in the province of Newfoundland and Labrador is the L'Anse Amour burial mound, which is situated on a high terrace overlooking the Strait of Belle Isle. Excavation revealed the skeleton of a twelve-year-old child buried approximately 7,500 years ago. It is the oldest known elaborate grave from the Americas. A wide variety of evidence was buried with this child, including a walrus tusk, a bird bone flute, spears made from caribou bone, a caribou antler pestle used to grind colourful minerals such as ochre and graphite for paints, a pendant, a decorated antler or ivory toggle, and a toggling harpoon used for hunting sea mammals. Fish bones were found in a fire pit that flanked the skeleton. From this assemblage of material and the placement of the grave looking out to the Strait, we can see that the short life of this child and the lives of those who buried him and left these gifts were deeply connected to both the land and the sea.

Other sites from the Straits region contain more ancient tools used specifically to hunt sea mammals. The sites demonstrate that the abundant ocean resources were becoming a primary focus for these early settlers. The majority of sites found in the region was located where boats could have been easily launched and landed; the artifacts recovered from these sites frequently contain gouges—a wood-working tool which is thought to have been used in the construction of watercraft such as dugout canoes. At the Fowler site, which is almost 7,000 years old, a fire pit was discovered that contained animal bones, including those of seal, caribou, and sea birds. These animals would have been accessible to hunters at different times of the year and it is possible that the early settlers were spending much of the year in and around their settlement locations. Nevertheless, by 7,500 years ago the inhabitants of southern Labrador were also venturing further from the Straits to explore the now accessible central coast of Labrador.

The climate and environment of Labrador continued to evolve and by 7,000 years ago the glaciers had completely retreated from the Labrador Peninsula. Warmer weather resulted in further changes to the Labrador landscape as lichen and shrub ground cover was replaced with birch, spruce, and fir forest which, while patchy in some regions, extended as far north as Okak, Labrador, around 5,500 years ago. North of Okak the cool climate prevented further

Seasonal Round

In the prehistoric period all of the different culture groups that occupied the province were hunter-gatherers. Hunter-gatherers have a subsistence economy based entirely on the acquisition of wild foods. Because they did not domesticate food sources to help them survive, they had to schedule their annual activities to take advantage of the wild food sources available in different locations at different times of the year. Generally speaking, these prehistoric culture groups took advantage of ocean resources in the spring through autumn when sea mammals, fish, sea birds, and shellfish were readily available. At this time berries and other plant foods were also harvested. During the summer months their sites were located along shorelines in both inner and outer bay regions as well as on islands. In the warm months food was plentiful and people could band together at larger settlements and visit relatives and friends. It was probably a very sociable time when social, political, and economic bonds were forged. In the colder winter months they split up into much smaller groups, perhaps nuclear families, and travelled to interior regions to hunt caribou and other smaller land mammals. Winter settlements were usually smaller than summer settlements because winter resources were less abundant and unlikely to feed as many people. Variations on this seasonal round depended on both the cultural traditions of each particular group and on the regions in which they lived. For example, the Paleo-eskimo populations, as well as the Thule, probably spent part of the winter months on the ice-edge hunting seals. Other groups, such as those that lived near Port au Choix on the Northern Peninsula, were situated to take advantage of the spring migration of harp seals close to their shores, and such abundance allowed them to live together in much larger groups for a longer period of time.

tree growth, so lichen and shrubs dominated the landscape. The human exploration of the central and northern reaches of Labrador almost parallels the development of the post-ice-age vegetation. By 7,000 years ago hunter-fishers occupied Hamilton Inlet and by 6,500 years ago they had travelled as far north as Ramah Bay, Labrador. The early sites from central and northern Labrador tell more about the daily life of these pioneers. Semi-subterranean houses ringed by large boulders were located on beach terraces that around 6,000 years ago would have been 2-3 metres above the shoreline; these now sit nearly 30 metres above the beach, well preserved for archaeologists to examine. These small houses, sometimes arranged in groups of two or three, provided comfortable living space for small nuclear families, indicating that local communities had small populations. Fire pits within the structures were used for heating and cooking. Cache pits found outside these houses were likely used for cold storage of foods. Similar to the archaeological sites in the Labrador Straits, these small communities were located near the shore to take advantage of abundant marine resources; the artifacts found in and near these houses suggest that caribou hunting remained an important activity. The first evidence that people had begun to explore and use the interior of Labrador also comes from this time. Several sites from the Mistastin and Boarder Beacon regions as well as a site located in northeastern Québec near

Ramah Chert

Ramah chert is a translucent, light grey, fine-grained quartzite that outcrops in the region of Ramah Bay in Northern Labrador. It is one of only two primary types of easily flaked lithic raw material that can be found in coastal Labrador; the other, Mugford chert, outcrops further south, just north of Nain. Ramah chert is visually distinctive and easily recognizable because of its colour, texture, and translucence. This raw material has been used by almost every Aboriginal group to inhabit Newfoundland and Labrador in the last 6,000 years to manufacture spear points and other tools. It was first used by the Labrador Archaic Indians, and continued to be used to varying degrees up to the period of European contact. Ramah chert occurs in archaeological sites at great distances from its source, as far south as New England and as far west as the upper St. Lawrence River valley; this indicates that it was a valued commodity and extensively traded. The reasons for this widespread trade may be due to the material's desirable flaking qualities, which help to produce fine quality, sharp stone tools. But probably equally important was its restricted geological distribution and its immediate recognizability, which made it an obviously "exotic" item and may have conferred prestige on individuals who had it.

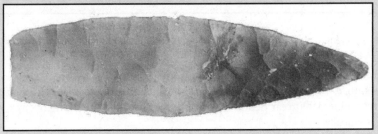

A lanceolate knife or spear point made of Ramah chert, from Porcupine Strand, southern Labrador (photo: P. Ramsden).

the Labrador border at Indian House Lake, a place where the George River caribou herd are known to cross the river, a perfect place for hunting, have been examined. Although further archaeological investigation is needed, it is possible that this pioneering population moved throughout the landscape in a seasonal cycle, affording them the opportunity to make the best use of the available resources in different locations. Coastal zones would have provided ample opportunity to hunt for sea mammals, fish, and sea birds between the late spring and early autumn. The interior provided good access to caribou herds during the cold weather months.

As these pioneers settled into the central and northern coasts of Labrador, they soon discovered a resource that would change their lives, one which would soon be desired throughout northeastern North America: a stone known as Ramah chert. This glassy rock was perfect for making the stone spear points and other implements used for hunting and domestic activities. It was a much easier material to shape into tools than most of the other sources they had encountered, with the added benefit of being a beautiful stone.

Red Paint Burials

In the area of Newfoundland and Labrador, Red Paint burials are associated with what is now known as the Maritime Archaic tradition, dating between 7,500 and 4,000 years ago. They are called Red Paint burials because of the characteristic use of red ochre (powdered, naturally occurring hematite) to sprinkle or paint the bodies or bones of those interred, and sometimes the accompanying artifacts, or as a grave inclusion in its own right. Similar burials are also associated with archaeological complexes of comparable age as far south as Maine, and are thought to be part of a widespread northeastern mortuary tradition. Although termed "burials," often no bones are found in the Red Paint features. In most cases, this might be because the bones have decayed in the acidic soil. However, it might also be that some of these features are ritual deposits of another sort, and never included human remains. Typically, the features include elaborate artifacts such as gouges, spear points (of chipped and ground stone), plummets, and, where preserved, a variety of bone implements and decorative or ritual objects. Recent research from Maine to Labrador has shown that the Archaic peoples who created the Red Paint burials had coastally adapted economies that included deep-sea hunting of sea mammals and swordfish.

This translucent quartz with shadings or bands of grey and black became the dominant material used in tool making. The first traces of this stone, or lithic, material make an appearance on archaeological sites in central Labrador about 6,500 years ago; by 3,500 years ago its use was widespread. During this intervening 3,000-year period the social organization of the settlers changed dramatically.

The first major change noted by archaeologists is the abandonment of southern Labrador south of Hamilton Inlet just over 6,000 years ago. Why these people chose to abandon their ancient homeland is not well understood, but it may be partially linked to their desire for Ramah chert. It was simply too far to travel between the Straits and Ramah Bay to collect this raw material for tool manufacture, especially when the foods and resources they had come to rely on in the south were also available in more northerly regions. The area between Hamilton Inlet and Nachvak Fiord became the focus of activity. People also abandoned their single family boulder houses for larger rectangular dwellings, which were segmented into separate household compartments but constructed for multiple family occupancy.

These dwellings are little more than rock outlines today, but, when occupied, they were probably tented with skins stretched over wooden frames. Between 4,000 and 3,500 years ago these longhouses became so exaggerated in size that they measured up to 80 metres in length and may have been occupied by fifty to 100 people at a time. At the archaeological site of Nulliak Cove in northern Labrador there are at least 27 of these house structures and, while they may not all have been occupied at one time, it is not unreasonable to suggest that several hundred people gathered together at this site regularly, most likely during the warm season. While there is no indication that people lived in

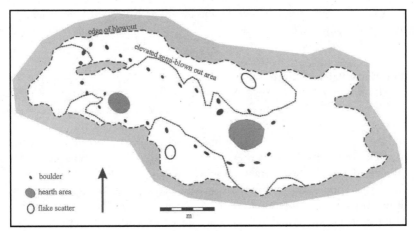

Plan of a Labrador Archaic longhouse, Upper Sandy Cove 3, southern shore of Groswater Bay (L. Rankin).

these structures year-round, the presence of such a large site implies that people were living at least part of the year in much larger groups than before. The population of the Labrador pioneers would have increased through time, but this may not have been the only reason that more people chose to live for at least part of the year in larger groups. During the summer months when travelling would have been somewhat easier, people probably gathered together to perform tasks that were best undertaken by a larger group, such as quarrying the substantial supplies of Ramah chert they now required. Bulk quantities of this stone would ultimately be taken back to settlements that were occupied by small family groups along the coast and into the interior during the rest of the year. The material could then be used to make tools, and excess quantities of the chert traded to groups who were unable to make it to the gatherings. In fact, both the raw material and shaped tools could be traded over very long distances, perhaps cementing relationships with distant groups. Tools made of Ramah chert have been recovered from archaeological sites as far away as New England, nearly 3,500 kilometres to the south.

Other activities were also best undertaken by a larger community. At Nulliak Cove there is evidence of caribou drive fences through which hunters, acting together, could herd caribou to force them toward opportune places for attack. Burying the dead and the mortuary rituals associated with this event appear to have been another element that was best undertaken at large gathering places. Mound burials like those constructed at L'Anse Amour and a newer form of cemetery burial were both used to memorialize the dead. Two large mound burials associated with the settlement at Nulliak Cove date between 3,500 and 4,000 years ago. A large variety of implements, including Ramah chert projectile points, red ochre, sheets of mica and birch bark, a native copper pendant, a walrus tusk, and a ground slate knife, were placed alongside the deceased. The size of the burials and the variety and quantity of beautiful objects placed in them suggest that many individuals contributed to memorializing the deceased.

The Early Paleo-eskimo

About 4,000 years ago the Labrador Archaic began to abandon their settlements in the far northern reaches of Labrador. Archaeologists are not certain why this occurred. Some have suggested that the climate was cooling and the far north was becoming less hospitable, but there is no direct evidence for this. Another significant event that occurred about this time may have influenced this decision: a new population began to colonize the northern landscape. This was an Arctic population of Paleo-eskimo, who were ethnically different from the Labrador Archaic. They were the first human inhabitants of most of the Arctic, and their colonization of the entire region from Alaska to Labrador took place rapidly, probably spanning only a few generations. For most of this epic journey, they were entering previously unoccupied territory, and, like Labrador's pioneers, they had probably never had to deal with any other group they were not related to by blood or marriage. This situation changed dramatically for both groups as the Paleo-eskimo turned down the Labrador coast. The Paleo-eskimo would first have become aware of the pioneers by finding their abandoned settlements. They seem to have used these abandoned communities as a way to help orient themselves in this new land by first moving into them and then exploring the terrain through forays to the south and west.

The Paleo-eskimo were historically, physically, culturally, and, no doubt, linguistically different from the pioneers. Having always lived in the Arctic world they had a very different tool which included harpoons tipped with serrated stone endblades, small projectile points, burins to engrave bone and wood, microblades for cutting, and various other scrapers, arrowheads, and adzes. Their houses were bilobate in form and separated into two sections by a passageway and hearth. These differences are easily recognizable to archaeologists. But for all their differences the Paleo-eskimo shared two important similarities with the pioneers: they were not familiar with different populations, and they relied heavily on the same natural resources. This may have made it difficult for the two populations to share the same territory; however, we don't know if the Labrador ecosystem would have been able to support two populations of hunters. The seemingly abundant resources in Labrador were always one step away from collapse. For example, a sleet storm could make fodder inaccessible and eradicate an entire caribou herd.

There is no direct archaeological evidence of any interaction, positive or negative, between the two groups, but we can see changes to the pioneers' way of life following the arrival of the Paleo-eskimo. It is at this time that their territory begins to shrink with the abandonment of their most northerly

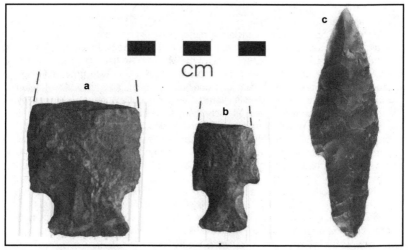

Spear points of the Maritime Archaic period from the Beaches site (a/b), and Labrador Archaic, collected at Sandy Cove, north end of the Porcupine Strand (c) (photos: a/b: J. Tuck, c: P. Ramsden).

settlements, the settlements that are maintained grow larger and their mortuary rituals become more elaborate. There are several reasons why these events may have occurred, but some archaeologists have suggested that these changes resulted from the stress placed on the founding population by the arrival of the new inhabitants. The pioneers, for example, may have started to gather in larger settlements to intimidate the new arrivals. By withdrawing from the north the pioneers may have been trying to move back towards their homelands in southern Labrador. However, any attempt to undertake this migration would have been blocked. During their lengthy absence from southern Labrador a second and distinct AmerIndian group had moved into the abandoned territory. Approximately 3,500 years ago, and after a colonization of Labrador that lasted over 5,000 years, the pioneers disappear from the records. It appears that with their territory squeezed at both ends they were unable to sustain their way of life. Like the mastodon, they appear to have gone extinct.

The First Settlers of Newfoundland

A new AmerIndian population moved into southern Labrador just over 6,000 years ago, as soon as the region had been abandoned by the pioneers and settled the region as far north as Groswater Bay. The artifacts they left behind were made quite differently than those of the pioneering population. Their projectile points were broadly notched in the side or had expanding stems and looked quite different from those manufactured by the pioneers. They also favoured different raw materials, including brown and white chert, for the production of these tools. As artifacts of similar form and manufacture

Port au Choix

At Port au Choix a series of ancient cemeteries dating between 3,300 and 4,400 years old are preserved by local alkaline soils and have helped archaeologists to understand much more about the lives of the Maritime Archaic. Over 117 human skeletons and four dogs have been excavated here along with grave offerings made of ochre and items made of stone, bone, antler, and ivory. The human remains indicate that many died in infancy. Surviving adults were generally healthy but experienced common traumas such as fractures to ribs and limbs. The bones also indicate that people engaged in much physical activity likely related to the procurement of food. The well-used artifacts buried here demonstrate the economic importance of marine resources. Long slate points and bayonets, as well as bone spears and barbed and toggling harpoons, would all have been used to hunt sea mammals.

Artistic renderings also represent the importance of the sea to the lives of those buried at Port au Choix. Two stone carvings depict images of killer whales. Seal and sea bird bones were used to decorate clothing and sea birds were frequently represented through carving. Nevertheless, land-based resources were also important. Bones and tools of caribou, eagle, hawk, owl, bear, otters, fox, and pine marten were all offered as burial gifts, and many finely made ground-stone tools show evidence of an extensive tradition of woodworking likely used in the manufacture of wooden implements, boats, and structures, even though none of these items have survived.

Strangely, the chipped stone points found at other sites used by these people are absent from the cemeteries at Port au Choix. These tools were most likely used to hunt caribou and other land mammals. Their absence suggests that these items were not considered suitable grave goods, perhaps because they failed to demonstrate the connection these people had to the sea, or perhaps they were simply considered too ubiquitous to be ceremonially deposited in a grave. The cemetery has been excavated by Dr. James Tuck of Memorial University and is interpreted by Parks Canada.

have been found along the St. Lawrence as far west as Québec City, this suggests that these new immigrants came from the west. Once in Labrador, however, the new immigrants seem to have settled into a way of life not unlike that of the pioneering population. Their camp sites were situated in almost identical locations to those chosen by the first population. While no house structures or animal remains have been found in association with these sites, we can assume from their locations and from our knowledge of species availability that this immigrant population had a similar maritime adaptation as their predecessors. We therefore refer to them as the Maritime Archaic Indians. Much more is known about this population from their sites on the island of Newfoundland.

The Maritime Archaic were the first people to occupy the island of Newfoundland. They came to the island approximately 5,000 years ago via the Strait of Belle Isle, perhaps in search of territory that was not available while the pioneers still occupied much of central and northern Labrador. It is possible that these people arrived on the island even earlier; sites on the

Northern Peninsula, the closest landfall to Labrador, may yet be found as archaeologists move further inland to examine ancient beach terraces from this period now located well interior from the current beaches. As much of the rest of the coast of Newfoundland is being submerged beneath the sea, earlier sites may now be under water. To date, the earliest site, at 5,000 years of age, is the Beaches site in Bonavista Bay. This site is disappearing beneath the ocean waves, but recovered artifacts indicate it was once a large habitation and workshop site where raw lithic material (rhyolite) was quarried and shaped into tools. Unfortunately, like many other important early sites on the island, such as those at Twillingate and Cow Head, there was no organic preservation and, therefore, we are unable to reconstruct many aspects of life. The preservation, however, is exceptional at Port au Choix, where a series of ancient burials has helped archaeologists to understand much more about the Maritime Archaic people.

By 3,300 years ago the last human remains were interred at the cemeteries of Port au Choix. By 3,200 years ago there was no further trace of the Maritime Archaic people. No one understands what happened to them. Perhaps they disappeared as a result of ecological circumstances: given the fragile nature of the Newfoundland ecosystem, small changes, even a threat to a single food resource, would substantially reduce the chances of survival for a hunter-gatherer population. Another possibility is that they withdrew to Labrador, where the population may have continued to thrive.

The Intermediate Indians

The AmerIndian occupation of the province between 3,200 and 2,000 years ago is poorly understood and, indeed, archaeologists cannot be certain whether the appearance of this Intermediate group is the result of a migration of yet another new population into the province or if it marks an adaptive change by Maritime Archaic still occupying southern Labrador. Certainly, the archaeological record changes significantly after 3,200 years ago. There are no more large burial complexes. Ground-stone woodworking tools, slate spears, and bayonets all disappear from the archaeological record. Yet there is reason to believe that the Intermediate Indians were the descendants of the Maritime Archaic population of southern Labrador. For one thing, there is no gap in the archaeological record to indicate a regional abandonment. For another, many tool types, like the distinctive broad-based, side-notched projectile points made from white chert, continue to be made. At the same time, new tools, such as small rectangular flake scrapers, are introduced to what appears to be a fairly traditional toolkit.

From the Strait of Belle Isle this Intermediate population appears to have spread north to the inner reaches of Groswater Bay and as far north as Okak for at least a few centuries during what appears to be a lull in the Paleo-eskimo occupation of the central and north coasts of Labrador. Tools recovered from

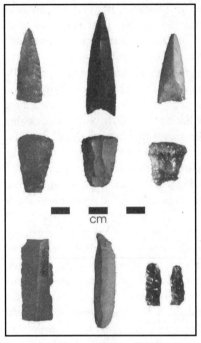

Dorset artifacts from Newfoundland. Top: harpoon end blades; middle: end scrapers; bottom: microblades. Artifacts on dark background are made of quartz (photos: J. Tuck).

sites in more northerly regions include the same side-notched projectile point style and the same distinctive scraper tool. But it is obvious that this population underwent some major changes through time. All of the sites associated with this culture are small, with very few artifacts, and show evidence of repeated seasonal occupation. Intermediate Indian sites have been found in places like North West River, Labrador, where no previous Maritime Archaic sites were located. A single Intermediate Indian artifact located on the island of Newfoundland suggests that the island was no longer significant to this population. Our best interpretation of the "Intermediate" culture pattern is that they occupied the Labrador coast during the summer months to take advantage of marine resources and moved to the Labrador interior during the winter where they developed a greater reliance on land mammals than had their ancestors.

This increased focus on interior resources may explain some of the changes to the toolkit at this time. The Ferguson Bay site in western Labrador is currently under excavation by Memorial University archaeologists. It is the first site in southwestern Labrador dating to this period to be completely excavated, and it is hoped that it will shed more light on the lives of these Intermediate occupants. Nevertheless, by 2,000 years ago even more dramatic changes occur.

The Dorset Paleo-eskimo

About 2,500 years ago the early Paleo-eskimo groups that inhabited Newfoundland and Labrador appeared to be slowly replaced by a new Paleo-eskimo culture known as the Dorset, who arrived from the north. The Dorset had a tool tradition distinct from earlier Paleo-eskimos that included tip-fluted harpoon end blades and large numbers of microblades. They chose to make their stone tools from the easily accessible Ramah chert. For the first time we see Paleo-eskimos taking advantage of the resources on the outer coast—something their predecessors did not do. For the first 500 years their settlements were confined to the northern Labrador coast, where they were best known from their occupation of Okak Bay. Here they occupied large rectangular houses at base camps in the inner islands during the winter months and made forays to the ice edge to hunt seal. In the spring they travelled to outer islands to hunt sea mammals. We remain uncertain how these people were occupied during the summer months, but they may have returned to inner island base camps in order to stage forays into the inner bay regions to hunt caribou and fish.

Soapstone bear, northern Labrador, c. AD 900 (photo: N. Pratt, courtesy of The Rooms Provincial Museum).

By 2,000 years ago Dorset sites were still thriving in northern Labrador and were sparsely distributed along the entire Labrador coast and on the island of Newfoundland. After reaching Newfoundland their population flourished. The well-preserved Phillip's Garden site located outside the town of Port au Choix on the Northern Peninsula contains at least fifty Dorset houses that were occupied between 2,000 and 1,200 years ago. While it is clear to archaeologists that not all of these houses were occupied at once, we do believe that many Dorset families came to Phillip's Garden each year to hunt harp seals that were readily available on the nearby pack ice during their migration north from their breeding grounds in the Gulf of St. Lawrence. This interpretation is well supported by refuse consisting of seal bones and sea mammal hunting implements found inside houses and surrounding middens. The abundance of seals to hunt provided an opportunity for the normally tiny camps of Dorset to gather together in one place. There is no doubt that this period provided great socializing, alliances and friendships could be renewed, and marriages between groups may well have taken place.

By 1,100 years ago the Dorset culture, with the largest population to inhabit the island in the prehistoric period, disappeared from Newfoundland. It is believed that the climate became much warmer during this period and likely affected the formation and distribution of sea ice and thus altered the ability of the Dorset to hunt the harp seal, which was the basis of their diet. With this resource no longer available, the Dorset of Newfoundland may have gone extinct or they may have decided to migrate to northern Labrador again, where conditions were more suitable for this arctic population.

Remnants of the Dorset culture are found in northern Labrador dating as recently as 500 years ago. After retreating to this region they were able to

---

Dorset Adaptations on the Island

As a population spreads through a landscape, it adapts to local conditions; so even though archaeologists may call a population by a single culture name, its material culture may exhibit regional differences. A good example is the Dorset population that occupied the island of Newfoundland between 2,000 and 1,100 years ago. Once on the island the Dorset Paleo-eskimo can be divided into three regional variants: the west coast Dorset, the northeast coast Dorset, and the southeast coast Dorset, each of which shares some common characteristics, but are nonetheless distinct. The west coast Dorset had an economy that was focused on the hunting of harp seal during their annual spring migration from the Gulf of St. Lawrence to the waters off Greenland. This rich and predictable resource allowed large numbers of Dorset people to live together for several months at the large site of Phillip's Garden in Port au Choix. The other Dorset populations on the island never gathered at such large settlements. The northeast coast Dorset also hunted harp seal, but probably not in the same numbers. As a result, they would have needed to access a greater variety of resources than the west coast Dorset, and we find their sites in many kinds of locations such as the outer coast and in inner bays where they no doubt spent more time hunting birds and land mammals as well as fishing for salmon. The Dorset occupying the southeast coast had no access to harp seal and, as a result, their economy was even more generalized. They occupied sites in the inner reaches of Trinity and Placentia Bays, often on small islands. From these home bases they hunted harbour seal and sea birds and must have made trips to the mainland for land mammal hunting. Perhaps because they did not hunt harp seal the Dorset culture in the southeast would not have been affected by changes in harp seal numbers and their generalized subsistence strategy allowed the Dorset in the southeast to inhabit the island much longer than the other groups. Further differences between each group are reflected in the way they manufactured tools. While they all made the same "types" of tools, they had access to different raw materials with which to make these tools, and each group produced a "local" variety of the tool which was distinct in each region. The differences between these groups are not so severe that archaeologists would suggest that they represent different culture groups, but they are strong enough to demonstrate that the Dorset, like many other prehistoric groups which inhabited the province, adapted to the different regions they chose to inhabit.

---

continue their traditional economic pattern focused on seal hunting for a few centuries before they, too, mysteriously disappear from the archaeological record, to be replaced by new immigrants.

The Recent Period Including the Inuit and Beothuk

Archaeologists begin to see changes in the AmerIndian culture pattern in the province about 2,000 years ago. The island of Newfoundland once again became a focus of settlement. However, there are many visible changes to the culture pattern in Labrador as well, including the locations of settlements, choice of raw material used to make tools, and the styles of artifacts. The changes appear to represent a new adaptation by resident peoples rather than the migration of a new culture group. This population, which inhabited Labrador 1,000 years ago, is known by archaeologists as the Point Revenge

A linear, raised hearth associated with the early Point Revenge culture (photo: S. Loring, courtesy of The Rooms Provincial Museum).

culture. Few of their sites have been excavated, but those which have, such as Winter Cove 4 in Hamilton Inlet, show an almost exclusive use of Ramah chert to manufacture notched projectile points and straight-based bifaces. On the central coast site of Kamarsuk, pottery has also been found. Few structures have been associated with this population, but an oval tent ring with a large central hearth excavated at Winter Cove 4 indicates that more than one family may have resided together. The location of sites indicates that much more use was being made of inner bay environments, and, when site location is combined with an analysis of material culture, it would appear that the Point Revenge people had a much more generalized economy than the earlier sea mammal hunters in the region.

Somewhere around 700 years ago sites representing this culture diminished on the coast. The population may have moved to the interior to avoid a new migratory population from northern Labrador. It is not yet fully understood if this group went extinct like so many other populations that came to this province or if they re-emerged some years later as the ancestors of the contemporary Labrador Innu. Further archaeological work in the interior of Labrador should resolve this issue.

Little is known about the population that came to the island of Newfoundland 2,000 years ago, but by 1,000 years ago a consistent culture pattern called "The Beaches" became apparent. These people are recognized largely by their tools, which include side-notched projectile points and large bifaces made of locally available rhyolite and cherts. Interestingly, one of these projectile points was found inside a Norse house at the L'Anse aux Meadows

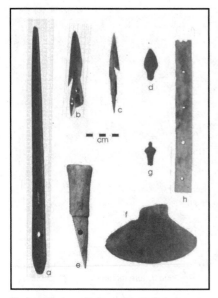

Thule artifacts: a: harpoon foreshaft; b: harpoon head; c: bone arrow point; d: slate harpoon blade; e: harpoon socket piece; f: stone ulu blade; g: wooden doll; h: bone sled shoe. Artifacts a, b, f, and h come from the Ikkusik site on Rose Island in Saglek Bay; artifacts c, d, e, and g are from various locations (photos: a/b/f/h: J. Tuck; c/d/e/g: P. Ramsden).

site on the Northern Peninsula. Their settlements, located in inner bays, suggest they had a generalized economy capable of taking advantage of a diversity of land and sea resources, and, as a result, the Recent Indians successfully expand into territories once exclusively occupied by the Dorset. At this time they start to produce smaller projectile points out of fine blue-green chert that resemble those made by their descendants—the Beothuk culture that inhabited the island when the Europeans arrived. Unfortunately, the Beothuk people did not survive their encounters with Europeans and went extinct in 1829.

A final wave of immigration occurred in northern Labrador approximately 600 years ago when people known as the Thule travelled to our shores from Baffin Island or Ungava Bay. These well-known Arctic whale hunters first restricted their settlement to northern Labrador, perhaps because a further expansion to the south was blocked by remnant Dorset settlement, but, soon after the Dorset disappeared, the Thule continued to migrate south at least as far as Sandwich Bay. They probably encountered the Recent Indians during this journey, but the two populations seemed to have divided into two separate territories to avoid each other. Thule settlements are concentrated on the north and central coast of Labrador, while the Recent Indians settled the interior and southern coast. The Thule continued their tradition of whale hunting after arriving in Labrador and supplemented this by hunting other marine mammals, fish, caribou, and birds—making use of all the resources Labrador had to offer. Their semi-subterranean winter houses and summer tent camps are littered with animal bones and other artifacts such as soapstone lamps, ground slate tools, small figurines, and ultimately European items.

By the early seventeenth century Thule settlements can be found as far south as Sandwich Bay, Labrador, where they regularly came into contact with European whalers and fishermen who occupied seasonal settlements on the southern coast. By this time the Inuit had been raiding these European camps for decades to acquire metal and other useful objects while the Europeans were absent and soon adopted these items into their toolkit. The descendants of Thule people, the Labrador Inuit, continue to call northern Labrador their home.

The prehistory of Newfoundland and Labrador is one of hopeful beginnings and tragic endings for many of the cultures who called this region home. The region offered the promise of abundant resources, but it was an ecosystem with a limited diversity of species. This ecosystem was so fragile that a small shift in climate or the growth of a population appears to have led to cultural extinctions and sudden evolutions in traditional culture patterns. Surely, this precarious prehistory resonates through the issues we face today.

Excavating an Inuit midden or refuse heap, associated with House 3 at Snack Cove, Huntingdon Island, Labrador (photo: L. Rankin).

Reconstructed turf houses at L'Anse aux Meadows (photo: B. Wallace, courtesy of Parks Canada).

The Norse at L'Anse aux Meadows
by Shannon Lewis-Simpson

In the nineteenth century the medieval Icelandic sagas *Grœnlandinga saga* and *Eíriks saga rauða* were translated into English, and a great amount of speculation and rumination was caused as to the precise location of *Helluland* (Slabland), *Markland* (Forest Land), and *Vínland* (Wineland). These places were thought to exist, if at all, in North America, and certainly west of Greenland, but where?

Despite other claims, the only excavated Norse site in North America is at L'Anse aux Meadows. Such finds as a spindle whorl and a copper alloy dress pin were recovered within and near eight buildings constructed at the site. Sufficient evidence was recovered to determine that the site was established probably by people from Greenland and Iceland. The site is radiocarbon dated to AD 1014, and has since been designated a UNESCO World Heritage Site and a National Historic Site.

One of the main reasons why the first excavator, Anne Stine Ingstad, originally decided to dig at L'Anse aux Meadows was that the site, filled with grassy meadows, looked like an attractive area for Viking-Age farmers to keep and feed domestic animals. For Ingstad, L'Anse aux Meadows fit into a preconceived notion of where a traditional Norse farmstead should be found. But, unlike at other Norse farmsteads, there is a total absence of evidence for animal husbandry at the site, nor are there any byres or outbuildings which one would expect on a farm. Instead, the eight structures formed four distinct complexes, with specific functions of woodworking, iron production, and smithing from local bog iron, and the production of iron boat nails. Although these activities are common at other Greenlandic and Icelandic farmsteads, their presence at L'Anse Aux Meadows in such a concentrated manner points to ship repair as being the main focus of the site and not farming, per se. There are sleeping areas for sixty-five to ninety people, considerably more than at any other contemporary farmstead in Greenland or Iceland; this suggests that more workers than usual were needed at this site. This is also suggestive of a degree of organization of the site's workers and resources to a common end and gives some indication as to the greater purpose for the site: that of a "gateway" settlement and a collection point for goods bound for Greenland and beyond, more than likely controlled by a single interest. The site was not occupied for one single period but many shorter periods for over a decade.

One of the prevailing myths concerning L'Anse aux Meadows is that the site was abandoned because of hostile interactions with a numerically superior indigenous population, a view largely formed from the saga accounts, which were written 300 to 400 years after the completion of any journey. It is more likely that several factors contributed to the site's disuse, chief of which was changing demographics in the North Atlantic region. As Parks Canada archaeologist Birgitta Wallace has suggested, the Greenland colony was too small to sustain expeditions to L'Anse aux Meadows and "the Norse expansion to the west had reached its practical limit."

Was there any link between this medieval Greenlandic exploration and later southern European voyages? To put it simply, we do not know. There is no extant archaeological or documentary evidence to support a continued Norse presence in Greenland past the middle of the fifteenth century. But in the fifteenth century English fishing fleets were increasingly active in Iceland, and it is known that some Icelandic vessels owned by families with English business interests did travel to Greenland in the late fourteenth and early fifteenth centuries. Some knowledge or remembrance of western lands was possibly passed on to fishing captains, but this did not amount to the precise sailing directions for other areas of the North Atlantic as used earlier by Viking-Age explorers.

Inside an Inuit Winter House c. 1600 at Snack Cove, Labrador

When they were not on the ice living in snow houses, the Inuit occupied semi-subterranean sod-dwellings between autumn and spring like those at Snack Cove on the southern Labrador coast excavated by Dr. Lisa Rankin of Memorial University. These houses, approximately 9 by 7 metres, were dug into the ground, and had timber-supported walls. Sods covered the timbers, and rocks held the sods in place. These houses were designed for warmth. One entered in a crouched position through a long entrance tunnel, at the end of which one stepped up onto the slab slate floor of the house interior. This step, called a cold trap, kept the cold air outside and the warm air inside. Inside the house each family maintained sleeping platforms at the sides and rear of the living space. The number of sleeping platforms informs archaeologists about the numbers of people living in the house. Most personal artifacts are found on and around the sleeping platforms. Close to the sleeping platforms archaeologists often find niches or even stone boxes where personal items were housed. Domestic activities like cooking, making tools, and socializing occurred in the centre of the floor. Stone lamps lit with seal oil were burnt for light, warmth, and cooking. The centre of the house is often littered with animal remains left over from meals and stone tools which were made, broken, and discarded or lost in the course of cooking and cleaning. These houses functioned so well in the cold Labrador winter that early European settlers to the coast were quick to adopt this style of architecture.

An excavated Inuit house at Snack Cove 3, Huntingdon Island, Labrador, looking from the back of the house across the paved floor and down the entrance passage (photo: L. Rankin).

Time Line

Culture Group	Location	Approximate Time Period
Labrador Archaic	Labrador	9,000 – 3,500 years ago
Maritime Archaic	Labrador	6,500 – 3,200 years ago
	Newfoundland	5,000 – 3,200 years ago
Intermediate Indian	Labrador	3,200 – 2,000 years ago
Recent Indians	Labrador	2,000 – 400 years ago
	Newfoundland	2,000 – 400 years ago
Pre-Dorset Paleo-eskimo	Labrador	4,100 – 3,500 years ago
Groswater Paleo-eskimo	Labrador	2,800 – 2,100 years ago
	Newfoundland	2,800 – 1,900 years ago
Dorset Paleo-eskimo	Labrador	2,500 – 700 years ago
	Newfoundland	2,000 – 1,100 years ago
Thule	Labrador	1,450 – 400 years ago

CHAPTER II

Newfoundland and Labrador, 1497-1697

Peter E. Pope

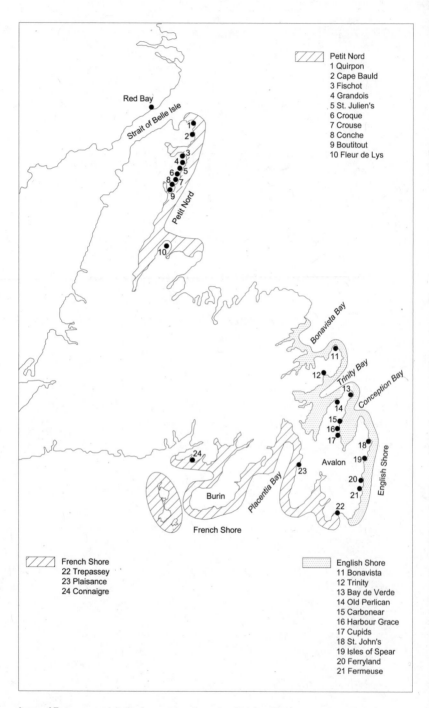

Areas of European exploitation in seventeenth-century Newfoundland.

For years, my neighbour Harry Maynard made a garden every May, somewhere in his pasture, with his horse, a handmade harness, and a wooden plough. His chickens followed, cleaning up the grubs. Every spring I planned to take a picture, but Harry inherited a tractor and abandoned his late medieval approach to raising vegetables before I got around to recording it. I did get a picture of Mike Wade's sod-roofed close-framed store on the Flatrock waterfront but that's gone as well, now. (To add insult to injury, the town banned this efficient form of roofing.) The trap skiffs, which until recently jostled for berths in the harbour every summer, were linear descendants of early modern hull forms, neither having much in common with the boxy and unstable longliners that have replaced them. Newfoundlanders of a certain age could be forgiven for supposing that the world of 1950 or even 1970 was, in some visible respects, closer to the world of 1650 than to the new millennium. The island took some major innovations on board between, say, 1700 and 1900—the Irish and with them the potato, then tea and later the cod trap, to name a few—but by 1700 parts of Newfoundland had already taken a form that is recognizable to those who can remember the world before frozen fish sticks.

The English Shore settlements along the east coast of the Avalon Peninsula and north to Trinity and Bonavista Bays, together with similar French establishments in Placentia Bay and around the Burin Peninsula, were innovations of the seventeenth century. These small societies served and were served by a larger sixteenth-century innovation, the transatlantic migratory fishery. In 1500 nothing like it had existed on this side of the Atlantic. In the 200 years following, Europeans took control of much of the island of Newfoundland, as well as the Strait of Belle Isle. For more than a century, this European presence was migratory and seasonal. In the seventeenth century, fisherfolk of Devon, Dorset, Breton, Norman, and Basque origins settled in Newfoundland and developed a way of life which endured into living memory.

For some writers, no history of Newfoundland is complete without fifteenth-century Bristol fishermen, pre-Colombian Basques, or even Norse refugees from late medieval Greenland. Such is the appeal of the exotic, that these shadowy figures rattle the gates of our historical consciousness. Should we let them in? It would be only prudent to examine their papers. When we do, we find that fifteenth-century Basque fishing expeditions to Newfoundland are the invention of eighteenth-century Spanish diplomats. There is no evidence at all for late-medieval Norse immigrants to Labrador; they are a superfluous hypothesis for the depopulation of the Norse colonies in Greenland. Only Bristol fishermen have anything resembling adequate late-medieval documentation but, in truth, even that is pretty thin. Some fishers from Bristol visited an island they had never seen before but could not say where it was and did not go back. Perhaps this was Labrador or even

Newfoundland or perhaps not. Short of further evidence, that visit remains moot and makes not much difference.

The Venetian Zuan Cabotto was the pilot who put Newfoundland on the map, in 1497. (This is the original Venetian form of the name of the man known to the English as John Cabot—he was never in his lifetime known as Giovanni.) Cabot might well have seen Labrador and he just might have seen Cape Breton; he certainly saw eastern Newfoundland, coasting between the Avalon Peninsula and Strait of Belle Isle. He departed for Bristol from Cape Bauld, only a few leagues from Leifr Eiríksson's exploration base. This is a thought-provoking coincidence, which raises the question of whether Cabot had tapped into the northern geographical tradition of lands to the west of Iceland. By 1500 or so, several Portuguese captains had visited our coasts as well, including Gaspar Corte Real, sailing out of Lisbon, and João Fernandes, a *lavrador* or Azorean land-holder. Fernandes's title eventually gave rise to the name "Labrador," although it remains uncertain whether the land he visited was the northern part of our province or perhaps, in fact, Greenland.

The Early Transatlantic Fishery

The immense fish stocks Cabot found impressed his crew. By 1502, the *Gabriel* of Bristol had made the first recorded transatlantic voyage to Newfoundland to salt and dry fish. Despite their sponsorship of these early voyages, it was not the English who developed this fishery, but captains and crews from the western European littoral between northern Portugal and the Channel Islands. By the late medieval period, this region was already a distinct and well-integrated transport zone, sharing a common shipping technology and knitted together by maritime trade. Within this economically integrated zone, word of a new fishery spread rapidly from the English and Azorean Portuguese involved in the first transatlantic ventures to their trading partners in northern Portugal, Bordeaux, Brittany, and Normandy. Their advanced navigation skills gave the Portuguese and the Bretons an advantage in exploiting the new industry and, by 1510, they were mounting transatlantic fishing expeditions. Norman crews were fishing in the New World by 1520 and the Basques by 1530. London and south coast ports like Southampton sent occasional ships to Newfoundland, but the English did not become significant players in the transatlantic fishery until after 1565, when they began the slow process of displacing the continental Europeans from the east coast of the Avalon Peninsula.

We get a flavour of early sixteenth-century Newfoundland from documents associated with the voyage of the *William* of London, which spent the summer of 1536 fishing at the Isles of Spear, off present-day Tor's Cove. So, at least one English crew was fishing here at this time. It is significant that the owner, William Dolphyn, chose to hire a Breton, one Alan Moyne, to act as a pilot on the voyage. It wasn't a very successful voyage for Dolphyn, who complained

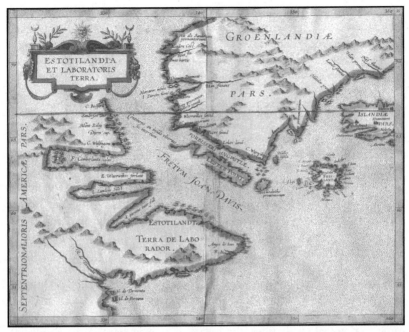

Descriptionis Ptolemaicae avgmentvm, siue occidentis notita breui commentario illustrata studio et opera Cornely Wytfliet Louaniensis (Lovanii: Tijpis Iohannis Bogardi, 1597, Centre for Newfoundland Studies).

in Admiralty Court that Moyne, who was also supposed to work as the ship's carpenter, spent the summer bowling and drinking with his countrymen. Breton activity at Newfoundland fishing stations is strongly supported in the archaeological record by the presence of distinctive coarse earthenware storage jars recovered from early contexts at Ferryland, St. John's, and on the northern Peninsula at Conche and Crouse. The Avalon Peninsula was not completely beyond the ken of English fishers in the early sixteenth century but the Newfoundland fishery remained a peripheral activity for the English, limited essentially to occasional voyages from London, Southampton, or Plymouth—sometimes, as in 1536, in cooperation with French merchants, masters, or pilots. Like the Portuguese, these occasional English crews seem generally to have confined themselves to the Avalon.

One of the enduring issues for the Newfoundland fishery emerged immediately. What would be the rules of competition for exploitation of an open access resource? Before the invention of geographical positioning systems, it was difficult to enclose the open sea, hence control of the land base for fishing became the key competitive issue. How could fishing crews, particularly fishing crews of different origins, agree to the allocation of fishing rooms—the shore spaces used to land, salt, and dry fish? Sometime before

1570, the admiral system had emerged as the answer to this dilemma. By this internationally recognized practice, the captain of the first ship arriving in a harbour became admiral and had first choice of fishing room; the second ship arriving had second choice; and so on. Fishers thus generally avoided costly and time-consuming squabbles about whose ship was biggest or which crew was most powerful.

Like all rules, the admiral system was sometimes ignored but the tone of outrage we hear in complaints about such behaviour suggests that this was a norm which almost everyone accepted. In the long term, the rule favoured larger ships, for the longer a ship was, the faster it could make its way through the water from Europe to Newfoundland. The average size of fishing ships grew over time, from 50 to 100 tons in the sixteenth century to 100 to 200 or even greater in the following century, though there was doubtless more than one reason for this. The admiral system also favoured transatlantic fishers from ports nearest Newfoundland. In the end, these were England's West Country ports: Poole, Topsham, Dartmouth, Plymouth, Bideford, and Barnstaple. Once they started to compete for fishing rooms on the Avalon, they had a locational advantage over their competitors. It is, perhaps, not just an accident that ships from Portugal's northern ports, Aveiro, Viana, and Porto, abandoned the Avalon in the same period that the West Country men came to dominate it. Besides, the towns of northeastern Portugal were by then developing more profitable voyages to Brazil.

The Basques, Bretons, and Normans of France paid renewed attention to the rest of Newfoundland and to other parts of Atlantic Canada. From about 1560, the Normans developed a Grand Banks fishery which, increasingly, absorbed their ships and men. The Bretons and Normans developed the Chapeau Rouge fishery on the Burin Peninsula, as well as fisheries in the Strait of Belle Isle, and along the Petit Nord, the Atlantic coast of the Great Northern Peninsula. The Basques fished almost everywhere but took a special interest in Placentia Bay, the Strait of Belle Isle and the Gulf of St. Lawrence, including Cape Breton, Gaspé, and Newfoundland's west coast. By the eighteenth century, the Bretons were concentrating on the Petit Nord in northeast Newfoundland and the Basques on the west coast of the island. In 200 years, European catches at Newfoundland grew from the few baskets of fish Cabot took to something like 200,000 to 250,000 tonnes, live catch. The British transatlantic fishery was responsible for only 25 per cent of this, about 50,000 metric tonnes a year. The French fishery was much bigger, taking 150,000 tonnes or more with about 50,000 tonnes by the Normans wet-salted on the Grand Banks and about 100,000 by shore-based fishing crews, mostly Basques and Bretons, salting and drying their catches on the fishing rooms of the south, west, and northeast coasts. In the later seventeenth century, the Breton fishery on the Petit Nord produced as much dry salt fish as the whole English Shore. The history of Newfoundland, to

Conche, Crouse, and Croque

The Atlantic coast of the Great Northern Peninsula was known in the seventeenth and eighteenth centuries as the Petit Nord. It was an important part of the French Shore, defined diplomatically by treaties after 1713. For Breton crews, it was already an important base for the inshore, migratory, seasonal, dry salt fishery. They had been coming to fishing stations like Fleur de Lys, Conche, Crouse, St. Julien's, Fischot, and Quirpon since the early sixteenth century. Archaeological surveys in the heart of this region, sponsored by the French Shore Historical Society, have identified many individual fishing rooms around Crouse, one of the harbours first used by migratory fishermen, and around Croque, for centuries the administrative centre of the French fishery. Dr. Peter Pope of Memorial University is excavating a traditional fishing room at Long Point, Crouse, once known as Champs Paya. Visitors can reach the site by hiking out a boardwalk from Crouse. The history and archaeology of the region are traced at the French Shore Interpretation Centre in Conche.

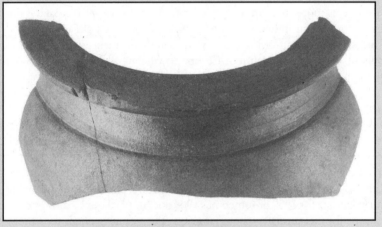

Rim of a Bessin-Cotentin Normandy Stoneware storage jar, excavated at Croque Waterfront. This is one of the most common types of ceramic vessel found on French fisheries sites of the seventeenth and eighteenth centuries (photo: Archaeology of the Petit Nord).

Innu or Beothuk scraper, flaked of European ballast flint, from surface collection on a beach in Grandois, EgAw-01. This is an artifact which dates itself: it must be post-contact (c. 1500) because it uses European material, and likely predates 1600 by which time Native people were scavenging European iron (photo: Archaeology of the Petit Nord).

> **Red Bay**
>
> In the sixteenth century, Red Bay, Labrador, was the Basque whaling station of Butus, according to the specialist in early Spanish documents, Selma Barkham. From about 1540 until the end of the century, thousands of Basques came every summer to the Labrador Straits to harpoon whales and to render them into oil. They shipped the oil back to Europe in casks, where it was used for soap, tanning leather, and lamps. By the 1580s, the population of northwest Atlantic right whales had been decimated and production fell off, particularly after the defeat of the Spanish Armada in 1588. The whaling station at Red Bay was excavated by Dr. James Tuck and a team from Memorial University and is now interpreted by Parks Canada. Robert Grenier and a team from Parks Canada excavated an important underwater wreck, probably the galleon *San Juan*, which sank in 1565. The National Historic Site where the Basque whaling industry in the Labrador Straits is interpreted has recently joined L'Anse aux Meadows as a UNESCO World Heritage Site.

this time, is more than the history of a few innovative settlements; it is also the history of an industry of world importance which already operated at a massive scale, employing tens of thousands of men every year, feeding millions of people in southern Europe by catching hundreds of thousands of tonnes of one species of fish.

Fisheries historians and biologists are still working on the complicated question of the long-term impact of fishers on fish stocks. A twofold consensus has emerged. First, the history of human predation must be understood as affecting ecological systems: human impact cannot be traced species by species. For example, human depletion of whale stocks around Spitzbergen in the European Arctic seems to have increased populations of some sea birds in the seventeenth century. Second, just because we have good statistical data for 1950 or sometimes 1900 does not make either an appropriate baseline for measuring ecological impacts. The virtual extinction of the right whale in the northwest Atlantic by Labrador-based Basques hunters in the late sixteenth century, the elimination of southern walrus populations about the same time, and predation on sea bird colonies by fishing crews gathering industrial quantities of bait all must have affected the marine ecosystems of the Atlantic coast, as much as the actual take in cod, massive as it was.

Early European Settlement

The sixteenth century saw the beginnings of population movement but no permanent changes to the existing settlement pattern which consisted of Inuit bands on the Labrador coast usually north of Sandwich Bay, ancestors of the Innu people in the Labrador Straits, and their relatives the Beothuk scattered around the island of Newfoundland, though apparently not on the Avalon south of Conception Bay. Some argue for intermittent Mi'kmaq visits to the south coast before European contact, although the evidence can also be read as suggesting that visits began in the sixteenth century. (The same might be said for Inuit visits to the Strait of Belle Isle.)

What about early European settlement? A shadow of evidence exists for a short-lived colony of Italian friars in Newfoundland in the late 1490s, possibly at Carbonear. (This is, at least, a fascinating idea, which deserves further research.) It is much more certain that an expedition of Azorean colonists came to Atlantic Canada in 1524. Although they visited southern Newfoundland, they moved on to Cape Breton to settle, perhaps at St. Peter's. The colony did not survive for long and was, perhaps, absorbed by the Mi'kmaq. Skeleton crews of Basque whalers sometimes over-wintered at Red Bay in the 1570s and 1580s, but these were not colonies. These were economic or climatic accidents: crewmen were paid to stay to make room for casks of whale oil processed

A 1567 woodcut of what is likely an advertisement for the exhibition of an Inuit woman and her daughter in the German city of Augsburg, who were captured by French sailors the year before. The text, in German, tells the readers that these are undoubtedly cannibals and advises them to thank God that they are not like that (from William Sturtevant, "The First Inuit Depiction by Europeans," *Etudes/Inuit Studies* 4, nos 1-2 [1980], 47-49).

in an especially productive season or, less happily, they were trapped by ice on the Labrador coast because they had stayed late into the fall in an effort to make a full cargo. Boosters of the British Empire cite Sir Humfrey Gilbert's visit to St. John's in 1583 as if it were the establishment of a colony, but this is blatant exaggeration. Gilbert was en route to Norumbega (that is, New England) to attempt settlement there; he called at St. John's to extort victuals from the fishing crews he knew he would find there. To this end, he ended up selling titles to fishing rooms. This had less to do with settlement than it did with lining Gilbert's pockets.

For about fifty years, say 1575-1625, Newfoundland became, at least, a topic of colonial speculation, if not yet of much actual action. By this time, Newfoundland had projectors, if not actual projects. Gilbert, for example, talked about a colony in Newfoundland during his 1583 visit. His lieutenant, Edward Hayes, survived the storm which drowned his commander, and

"Descriptio Terrae Novae," from *P. Bertii Tabvlarvm geographicarvm contractarvm libri quinque* (Amsterdam: C. Nicolai, 1602, or 1606, Centre for Newfoundland Studies).

Was Newfoundland Britain's Oldest Colony?

Not really. In a way Britain's oldest colony was Ireland, colonized by the English in the High Middle Ages and recolonized in the late sixteenth century. Among overseas colonies, Virginia was permanently settled in 1607, three years before Newfoundland in 1610. It is true that Sir Humfrey Gilbert claimed Newfoundland for Britain in 1583, but there was no settlement at that time.

Is St. John's the Oldest City in North America?

By North American standards, St. John's is an old European settlement but it is hard to accept the traditional local claim that it is the oldest. Mexico City was a metropolis of hundreds of thousands of people well before Europeans arrived in North America. In the present US, St. Augustine, Florida, was settled in 1565 and in present-day Canada, Québec City was settled in 1608. St. John's was not settled until sometime between 1610 and 1620. We might claim St. John's as the oldest European harbour in North America—it was certainly in use before 1519—but only at the expense of ignoring other early seasonal fishing stations in Newfoundland and Labrador, like Chateau, Quirpon, Ferryland, or Fermeuse. But Water Street might be the oldest European street in North America, for it follows the original fisherman's beach path.

tells us that in the end Gilbert became "a northern man," as optimistic about settlement here as in the more recently discovered Norumbega. In 1578, Anthony Parkhurst had already written a proposal for settlement of Newfoundland and Hayes wrote another, to be followed by John Mason, Sir Richard Whitbourne, Edward Wynne, and others in the early seventeenth century. Parallel schemes for settlement of Acadia and the St. Lawrence were mooted in France and a short-lived colony of convicts was even planted on Sable Island. It would be no exaggeration but only a provocative truth to observe that the oldest literary form in Canada is the funding proposal.

Europe sent its first successful colonists to North America, in a wave of dispersion, during the first quarter of the seventeenth century. These were the colonies whose establishment we have begun to celebrate 400 years later, at the turn of the twenty-first century: Acadia (1604), Maine (1605), Jamestown, Virginia (1607), Québec (1608), Cupids (1610), Bermuda (1612), Plymouth (1620), Ferryland (1621), and others, less memorable, if not less significant. This flurry of activity by companies set up in England and France to invest in the colonization of North America followed closely at the end of a long European war. It was as if investors had already made up their minds that this was a promising speculation and, once a truce eliminated the insecurity of maritime war, commercially sponsored colonization followed.

The Newfoundland Company, a chartered limited-stock company set up by London and Bristol merchants to establish a colony, was typical of these ventures—in fact some of its shareholders were also shareholders in the Virginia and the Bermuda companies. In 1610, John Guy arrived at Cupids with a small band of colonists, who erected a sturdy west-country style house, now uncovered by archaeologists. In 1612, Guy himself went back to Bristol to carry on a distinguished career as a merchant, mayor, and Member of Parliament. The colony survived and even grew, with the arrival of sixteen women in 1612 and the birth of a child to Guy's nephew Nicholas and his wife in 1613. The company, on the other hand, did not do so well, while the colony seems to have drifted economically, burdened with too many gentlemen "who scorned to turne a fish," as manager Henry Crout put it. The colony suffered the depredations of the celebrated pirate Peter Easton, who shook them down for badly needed livestock, only to suffer a very cold season in the ensuing winter of 1613. The Bristol investors regrouped by sponsoring resettlement at Harbour Grace. Historians have traditionally assumed that the original Cupids colony then faded away, but the archaeology of the site indicates pretty clearly that it was permanently inhabited until about 1665 when it was burned, probably during the Dutch raid on the English Shore. In the end, Cupids was a productive colony, even if it did not turn a profit for its investors. It brought the first European settlers to Conception Bay, and spawned a number of other colonial investments over the next decade as the original investors sold off lots to other interests.

Cupids

Cupids or Cuper's Cove was already known as a fishing station in 1610 when John Guy and a small band of colonists founded the first permanent English settlement in what is now Canada. In 1613, Nicholas Guy's wife delivered the first historically documented European child born in Canada. Their son lived a long life for his passing was remembered by settlers who spoke to the French chaplain, Father Beaudoin, at the very end of the century. Like the Guys, most settlers from Cupids moved to other settlements in Conception Bay, like Harbour Grace and Carbonear. Cupids itself was still occupied late in the seventeenth century, although it was burned by the Dutch in 1665. By the 1670s it may have been a winter home for the Butlers of Port de Grave. Archaeologist Bill Gilbert identified Guy's original settlement through brilliant documentary detective work and is now interpreting the site for the Baccalieu Trail Heritage Corporation.

Ferryland

Ferryland was one of the fishing stations developed by the Portuguese in the early sixteenth century. Archaeological finds suggest regular use by Breton fishers about 1550. West Country fishers displaced them in the later sixteenth century before Sir George Calvert, Lord Baltimore, sent colonists under Captain Edward Wynne to found a colony in 1621. Ferryland was the centre of Calvert's Province of Avalon (1621-1629) and also the commercial base of Sir David Kirke's later Newfoundland Plantation (1638-1651). Sir David's widow, Lady Sara Kirke, and her sons dominated the local scene until the end of the century. Archaeologists have found a wealth of material from both the Calvert and Kirke periods. Ferryland has been continuously inhabited since 1621, except for the terrible winter of 1697, just after the French attack. Archaeological interpretation of the early settlement, by Dr. James Tuck and Dr. Barry Gaulton of Memorial University, is sponsored by the Colony of Avalon Foundation.

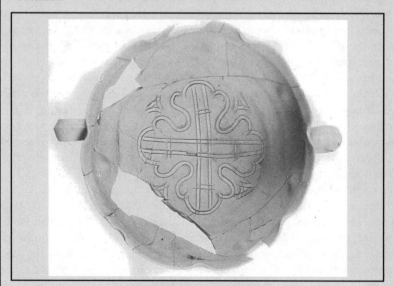

Portuguese *terra sigillata* bowl, Ferryland (photo: B. Gaulton).

The most important of these was the Province of Avalon, which consisted of a swathe of territory across the peninsula, between Renews and Petty Harbour, granted in 1621 by James I to his sometime Secretary of State, Sir George Calvert, later first Baron Baltimore. Calvert made a large investment in a colony at Ferryland, site of the celebrated archaeological site known today as the Colony of Avalon (not a name used in the seventeenth century). Baltimore even came out to Ferryland with his wife and a baronial retinue of about forty retainers to spend a year here in 1628-1629. That was another cold winter, too cold for Lady Calvert, and the family moved on, Baltimore famously telling Charles I that he would "committ this place to fishermen that are able to encounter storms and hard weather." Sir George managed to wangle a new grant in the Chesapeake, and, although he did not live to see it, his family would found Maryland. That state has claimed to be the first non- or, at least, multi-denominational colony in North America, but that distinction really belongs to the Province of Avalon. On his retirement from politics in 1625, Calvert reverted to Roman Catholicism and was concerned to make a place for his co-religionists in the New World. The Crown was certainly not going to permit a colony restricted to Roman Catholics but it was willing to let Calvert broaden the acceptable pool of emigrants from those willing to accept the thirty-nine articles of the established Church of England. When the Calverts departed the Province of Avalon, they left about thirty settlers around Ferryland and these families were among the founder settlers of the Southern Shore.

Permanent settlement in Ferryland and indeed along the English Shore got an important boost with the establishment of the Newfoundland Plantation: a project for commercial exploitation of the Newfoundland fishery under a patent granted in 1637 by Charles I to Sir David Kirke and a syndicate of powerful courtiers.

The Grant of Newfoundland gave Kirke's syndicate a trading monopoly with powers to tax foreign fishers and traders, even as it restricted (on paper) rights to property in Newfoundland. The patentees invited Kirke, Berkeley, and company to manage the project. This was a London trading house, active in the 1630s and 1640s, consisting of a partnership of three of the Kirke brothers—James, John, and David—with Sir William Berkeley, who had originally gone into business with their father, Gervaise.

Sir David Kirke

Sir David Kirke was an amusing, ambitious, and aggressive, even ruthless, businessman. Think of Conrad Black in lace, with a sword. He made his Newfoundland adventure pay and did so from the base he established in Ferryland, literally building on the foundations laid by Calvert's foreman, Edward Wynne. Sir David Kirke was Newfoundland's first resident governor. He is not usually remembered this way, essentially because he was not a naval

Newfoundland coat of arms granted to Sir David Kirke, 1638, officially adopted as Newfoundland and Labrador's coat of arms in the 1920s (courtesy of the College of Arms, Misc. Grants 4.7, from Peter Neary and Patrick O'Flaherty, *Part of the Main: An Illustrated History of Newfoundland and Labrador* [St. John's, Newfoundland: Breakwater Books, 1983]).

governor in the mould of the captains and commodores who were styled governors of Newfoundland in the eighteenth century. Kirke held courts, licensed taverns, and collected taxes: he behaved like a governor and was so regarded by his contemporaries between 1638 and 1651.

Perhaps more importantly, Sir David Kirke was Newfoundland's first resident fish merchant. The business empire of Kirke, Berkeley, and company spanned the Atlantic from London to Ferryland, to Boston, France, and Spain. Sir David bought several small New England ships, which he operated out of Ferryland. These likely included *The Lady*, named after his wife, the redoubtable Lady Sara Kirke. We don't know where he sold his fish, but archaeological remains of the fine ceramics collected by Lady Kirke after she was widowed include exotic Portuguese wares, among them colourful *faiança* dishes and pseudo-classical *terra sigillata*. By the mid-seventeenth century, the Portuguese were great buyers of dry salt cod rather than great producers and the northern towns of Aveiro, Porto, and Viana were likely markets for the Kirkes and their competitors in Newfoundland and New England.

Like his successors, Kirke made as much money importing goods for a clientele of dependent fish-processing families as he did by exporting cargoes of dry salt cod. Kirke, Berkeley, and company flourished during the 1640s, when Sir David Kirke financed the first regular trading links between Newfoundland and New England. Kirke's books have not survived and his references to his own finances have all the clarity of a press release from Enron. It is impossible to prove, then, that the patron-client credit relations later known as the "truck" system were already developed on the English Shore. Impossible to prove but certainly likely: by the end of the century Newfoundland planters were, as Governor Pasteur de Costebelle of Placentia delicately put it, married to their merchant by what he called "la commerce de la troque." Sir David Kirke's widow and sons dominated the economy of the South Avalon through the second half of the seventeenth century, and they certainly relied on carefully controlled credit to do this. Others likely played the same role elsewhere on the English Shore: Oxfords and Downings in St. John's; Pinns, Guys, and Butlers in Conception Bay; Taverners and Baileys north of Bay de Verde.

Newfoundland after 1660

Resident merchants could prosper, of course, only because informal settlement in the half-century from 1630 to 1680 had created a population of fisherfolk, scattered in about thirty hamlets between Bonavista and Trepassey. Some of the more important centres, Harbour Grace and St. John's for example, had loose connections with the proprietary investments of the first quarter of

The *Sapphire*, sunk by French forces at Bay Bulls in 1696.

the century but by 1640 they were proprietary colonies no more. The English Civil War (1641-1649) may have encouraged emigration, even as it disrupted normal patterns of shipping and provided new economic opportunities in the North American colonies. By 1660, the Newfoundland planters numbered perhaps 1,500 souls, over-wintering servants included, and by 1680 probably approached 2,000. (To give some perspective, Acadia had about the same European population at the time and Québec was just beginning to expand from this level.) Ferryland remained the effective capital of the island, even after Parliament's victory, the execution of Charles and the establishment of the Commonwealth (1649-1653), when Kirke was recalled to London, to face legal problems, imprisonment, sickness, and death. But Newfoundland's future lay elsewhere.

By 1675, when Captain Sir John Berry took the first comprehensive census of the English Shore, St. John's was already by far the largest settlement in Newfoundland, with an over-wintering population of about 200—that is, about twice its closest competitors of Ferryland, Carbonear, Bay de Verde, Old Perlican, and Bonavista.

The population of St. John's swelled spectacularly every summer. From its earliest days, St. John's was a major centre for the seasonal migratory fishery, and its annual peak in this period was about 2,500 people—one of the largest concentrations of Europeans north of Boston. Conception Bay was probably richer, taken as a whole. It had the advantage of livestock agriculture and accessible timber. Some planters there were reputed to be worth £1,000, a

Placentia

Placentia or Plaisance was an important seasonal fishing station for the Basques long before it was first permanently settled by Basque, Breton, and Norman fisherfolk in the early 1660s. From its inception it was a fortified settlement and rapidly became the capital of the French Shore. Devastated by raiders from Ferryland in 1694, it was rebuilt by the French and successfully defended until 1713. Then, by the Treaty of Utrecht, France agreed to give up permanent settlements in Newfoundland. Amanda Crompton of Memorial University excavated the Vieux Fort, dating about 1662-1685. The site of this fortified house can be visited by boat, from present-day Placentia. Parks Canada's site at Castle Hill is essentially eighteenth century, as is Fort St. Louis, an archaeological project sponsored by the Placentia Historical Society.

respectable fortune in this period. Bonavista was also growing, as were Bay de Verde and Trinity.

About 1662, the French established an over-wintering colony in Placentia. After a few hard years and a bloody mutiny, this settlement found a way to survive in much the same way as the English Shore. Resident fisherfolk, most of them families with children, employed transient servants to harvest and cure fish, which they marketed through local merchants, who had the necessary transatlantic connections. These families supplemented their income by providing hospitality to the seasonal fishing crews who arrived every summer from metropolitan ports—hospitality consisting of shelter from the storm and as much wine, spirits, and tobacco as a friendly advance on shares in fish would allow. By the end of the century, Plaisance was almost as well populated as St. John's. Its penumbra of dependent outports was smaller than the latter's, but French settlement stretched from Trepassey, across Placentia Bay to the Burin Peninsula and even to Harbour Breton and Connaigre. Placentia's merchants were enmeshed in the developing network of colonial trade linking Québec and France itself and they seem to have found it no less profitable to trade with the same New England merchants who came annually to sell their clapboards and molasses and rum along the English Shore. After the outbreak of war at the end of the century, they also developed a sideline in privateering. But until the breakdown of relations between Britain and France after 1688, relations between their settlers in Newfoundland were usually civil, sometimes cordial and often mutually profitable. Neither of these two small societies paid much attention to the even smaller bands of Beothuk, scattered on the northeast coast, except when Native scavenging extended beyond seasonally abandoned fishing stations. On the other hand, the French were regularly involved with the Mi'kmaq, who were willing to travel considerable distances to trade at Plaisance. Meanwhile, a seasonal guerrilla war flared between the Inuit and Breton fishermen, at their seasonal fishing stations on the Petit Nord.

Government

Placentia, as a crown colony under a state-appointed military governor, had a more transparent form of administration than the English Shore, even if the French governors were corrupt, beyond the expectations of their time. In the 1650s, the Council of State had appointed the Newfoundland Commissioners to look into Kirke's operations and to attend to the Commonwealth's affairs here. Revolutionary upheaval thus permitted Dartmouth interests, personified by the Maine trader John Treworgie, to wrest control of the Newfoundland trade from Kirke, Berkeley, and company. The Newfoundland Commissioners were, in fact, competitors of the Kirkes who harboured previous commercial grudges. They do not actually seem to have governed much, any more than the agents of

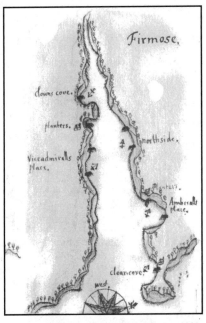

James Yonge, Fermeuse (Firmose), c. 1663, depicting, clockwise: "viceadmiralls place; planters; clowns cove; northside; planters; Amboralls place; clear cove" (courtesy of the Plymouth Athenaeum).

the Calverts who were briefly restored to a paper proprietorship in the early 1660s after the Restoration of Charles II.

The administration of the migratory fishery remained the responsibility of the fishing admirals. The Western Charters were royal patents granted in 1634, 1661, and 1676 to the West Country ports seasonally involved in the fishery on the English Shore. They prescribed how migratory fishing masters could claim fishing rooms and reiterated the traditional customs of the fishery, including the power of fishing admirals to settle disputes. After Kirke's demise, other disputes could only be settled in Admiralty Court, in London or Exeter or Boston. If a will was to be registered or go to probate, that too would have to be done in a distant court. Planters could not even solemnize a marriage or baptize their children unless a Royal Navy chaplain happened to visit during a summer tour of duty. The naval state, a colony administered by the Royal Navy, was beginning to emerge, but the English Shore in the late seventeenth century remained an anomaly: a civil society essentially without local government.

The growth of colonial and military bureaucracies in London and Paris from about 1660 on has left us with denser documentation of Newfoundland

	Migratory Fishing Crews	Seventeenth-Century Planters
January	Assemble crews	Furring and scavenging expeditions (by servants for planters)
February	Crews assembled; ships depart European ports	Lumbering and boat building
March	Ships depart European ports	
April	Sack ships set sail	
May	Crews arrive and take fishing rooms	Host early migratory crews; sell boats and timber
June	Crews arrive and take fishing rooms; boat repair or purchase from planters; cut timber and build stages, etc.; fish capelin for bait	Gardening and prepare own boats; sell boats and timber, build stages, etc.; hospitality industry; fish capelin for bait
July	Cod fishery and load sack ships	Cod fishery and load sack ships; hospitality industry
August	Cod fishery and load sack ships for voyage home	Cod fishery and load sack ships; cut wood or recycle stages, etc.; hospitality industry
September	Fishing ships bring crews home; sack ships deliver salt cod to southern Europe	Store boats for migratory crews; fall fishery, harvest berries
October	Sack ships deliver salt cod to southern Europe	Fall fishery, store vegetables
November	Sack ships deliver wine, oil, and fruit to northern Europe	Slaughter livestock
December		Furring and scavenging expeditions (by servants for planters)

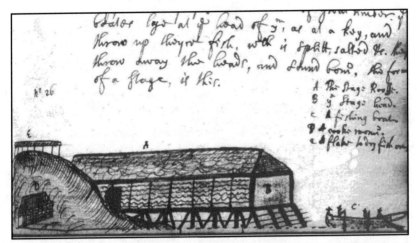

James Yonge, "A View of a Stage and Also of the Manner of Fishing for, Curing, and Drying Cod at New Found Land," c. 1663. A) the stage room; B) the stage head; C) a fishing boat; D) a cook room; E) a flake to dry fish on (courtesy of the Plymouth Athenaeum).

in this period than for preceding ones. Surveys of French fishing rooms record in some detail the consolidation of migratory fisheries on the Chapeau Rouge and the Petit Nord. Plaisance and its nearby outports are documented in early census records of the 1670s, 1680s, and 1690s, although we have to sketch in the history of the Basque west coast from more peripheral sources. The celebrated Replies to Heads of Inquiries, filed by the Royal Navy commodores of Britain's Newfoundland station from 1675 on, comprise some of the earliest census records for any British jurisdiction and contain a surprising wealth of socio-economic data: heads of households, wives, children, servants, fishing rooms, boats, train oil vats, even (sometimes) cows, pigs, and gardens. These detailed reports also include discussion of key administrative issues and from these papers we get a sense of the major problems facing the colony that was not quite a colony. These included the establishment of resident fisherfolk, which some argued had reduced fish stocks; violence in the fishery among crews competing for rooms; and conflict or potential conflict with the French.

Conflict

By 1680, the resident fisherfolk of the English Shore were taking about a third of the total British catch of cod at Newfoundland. Since the number of migratory crews had fallen during wars with Spain and with the Netherlands between the 1650s and the 1670s, it is hard to accept uncritically the view of some contemporary West Country interests that the Newfoundland planters were depleting stocks. The make-up of the British fishery at Newfoundland was simply changing. In 1681, catches fell by about half, a crisis which

The Myth of Illegal Settlement

This myth was born when nineteenth-century historians exaggerated eighteenth-century restrictions and projected them back into the seventeenth century. Newfoundland planters of that time did not think of themselves as living illegally here. Sir David Kirke and his partners in the 1640s must have been aware that their patent denied them title to property within 4 miles of the Atlantic. This did not prevent them from settling and building on the coast, any more than similar paper restrictions later in the century affected planters of that period. It is true that Captain John Berry arrived in St. John's in 1675 with instructions for the planters to leave, but he judiciously decided against applying this policy. If possession is nine parts of the law, then settlement was never effectively illegal in seventeenth-century Newfoundland. Over-wintering on the French Shore of the eighteenth century, by either French or British subjects, was banned in 1713 by the Treaty of Utrecht. That rule was applied rigorously to the French after 1763 but rarely seriously affected English settlement. Irish Catholics were deliberately discouraged from settling by Governor Palliser in the 1760s but this prejudice was only erratically imposed and usually on the destitute. These more serious eighteenth-century restrictions did not exist in the seventeenth century.

contemporaries blamed on overfishing. Since this period also saw a distinct climatic cooling, with stormy weather and more frequent sea ice, other pressures may also have affected access to cod stocks. Whatever the factors which contributed to the decline in catches, migratory fishing masters could fish elsewhere and many seem to have done so for several years. Fishers resident in Newfoundland had no such option and so, inevitably, took a relatively larger share even as total catches fell. Stocks did not fully recover until after the outbreak of war in 1689. As usual, war reduced participation in the transatlantic fishery and these years of reduced effort saw spectacular catches among both French and British fishers, migratory and resident.

With the Restoration of 1660 and the gradual re-expansion of the West Country migratory fishery came the first significant conflicts over resources between Newfoundland's migratory and resident fishers. Conflict in the fishery was endemic, as fishers competed for fishing rooms every summer. Historians have sometimes over-specified such competition, as if it existed only between planters and ship-based migratory fishing crews. In fact, masters complained frequently about unfair practices within the migratory fishery—which is to say that the practice of the admiral system was continually contested. At various scales, bye-boat keepers competed with ship-masters, Barnstaple competed with Bideford, North Devon with South Devon, Devon crews with Dorset crews, and English crews with French and even, by the end of the century, with Irish crews. It is fairer to see this competition as fisher versus fisher. Planter-migratory competition was, however, part of this story; for example, when a Dartmouth crew burned Thomas Oxford's rooms at St. John's in the 1670s. Planter-migratory competition was easy to politicize, and politicization of this conflict in the 1670s fed into the complex history of rules about Newfoundland settlement. Although Newfoundlanders have taken the myth of illegal settlement as their own, that myth has only a limited truth—a truth which reflects an eighteenth-century reality rather than a seventeenth-century one. Intense lobbying by an anti-planter faction in the West Country and some judicious bribery briefly persuaded Whitehall to attempt to discourage settlement for a few years in the mid-1670s. But Britain normally permitted and often encouraged settlement of the English Shore in the seventeenth century.

The seriousness with which France and Britain contested Newfoundland at the end of the century is a clear indication of the value of not only their fisheries but also of their quasi-colonies. The war arose from European tensions, following the Glorious Revolution of 1688, which put the Protestants William of Orange and Queen Mary on the British throne in place of the Roman Catholic Stuart heir, James II. It was only a question of months until the France of Louis XIV was at war with an increasingly aggressive Protestant Britain. Amicable relations broke down more slowly in Newfoundland. The settlers of the English Shore opened an exchange of vicious raids, by sacking Plaisance in 1694. This particular bout ended in 1697, with the complete destruction of the settlements of the English Shore and the exile of almost all the English planters who had not died in combat or in detention. Why the deportation of the Newfoundlanders remains a footnote in Canadian history is a good question. This episode was as significant in its time as the exile of the Acadians a half-century later. One factor may be that Newfoundlanders were not yet a self-conscious ethnic group, in the sense that the Acadians were by 1752. The Newfoundland exile is also obscured by the myth of illegal settlement, which prefers to find limits on early settlement in London or the West Country, rather than in Paris or Québec.

The English Shore was, in fact, rapidly resettled—which is, itself, a very clear indication both of Britain's effective settlement policy and of the economic importance of the planters to the migratory fishery. The dispersal of Newfoundland's English settlements in 1697 has tended to make them seem, in retrospect, temporary. Some scholars have even characterized English settlement in seventeenth-century Newfoundland as impermanent. Census data from the period belie this claim. The Newfoundland planters were no less likely to move than householders in most other regions around the North Atlantic. Their servants were relatively mobile, as were working people everywhere in the maritime world. In this sense, even if they were specialized, Newfoundland's English and French Shores were normal parts of the seventeenth-century North Atlantic world.

"View from a platform [stage], and of the manner in which salt cod is fished, prepared, and dried in Newfoundland." a) "Fisherman's suit"; b) "The rope with the fish-hook"; c) "The manner of fishing"; d) "Men who are preparing the fish"; e) "Trough where they throw the fish when it is ready"; f) "Case of brine"; g) "Manner of carrying it"; h) "Manner of cleaning it"; i) "Press to extract the oil from the cod livers"; k) "Barrel that receives the water and the blood of the livers"; l) "Other barrel that receives the oil"; m) "Manner of drying the fish," c. 1763. This is an Italian version of an engraving depicting the operation of the Newfoundland fishery in the early eighteenth century; there are also English and French versions (courtesy of the Centre for Newfoundland Studies).

Time Line

c. 1000	The Greenlander Leifr Eiríksson builds an exploration base camp in the Strait of Belle Isle.
c. 1340	Last known Greenlandic voyages to Labrador.
1497	Zuan Cabotto explores east coast of Newfoundland.
1499	João Fernandes explores the coast of Greenland (and Labrador?).
1500-1501	Gaspar Corte Real explores the coast of Newfoundland (and Labrador?).
1502	The *Gabriel* of Bristol makes the first recorded fishing voyage to Newfoundland but the English fishery at Newfoundland is not significant until about 1565.
1504	First recorded French fishing voyage to Newfoundland.
1506	Portuguese tax cod from Newfoundland.
1508	Sebastian Cabot explores the Labrador coast.
1510	First recorded Breton fishing voyage to Newfoundland.
1511	First recorded Basque fishing voyage to Newfoundland (with a Breton pilot).
1527	Of fourteen ships fishing at St. John's, eleven were Norman, two Portuguese, and one Breton.
1534	Jacques Cartier sails through the Strait of Belle Isle into the Gulf of St. Lawrence, where he meets French fishing ships.
1535	Cartier circumnavigates Newfoundland, establishing its insular character.
1536	First recorded transatlantic tourist venture (from London) ends in disaster off Labrador. Breton crews pass time at the Isles of Spear (Tors Cove) bowling—was this the first European sport to reach Canada?
c. 1540	Spanish Basques organize whaling voyages to the Grand Bay (Strait of Belle Isle).
1541	Bretons and Basques fishing at Crouse provision Cartier on his third voyage.
1550s	Open warfare between French and Spanish Basque vessels at Newfoundland.

1559	Treaty of Cateau-Cambrésis between France and Spain shifts European alliances and the English begin to compete seriously in the migratory fishery at Newfoundland.
c. 1575	Basque whalers over-winter at Red Bay, Labrador.
1579	Basque Miguel de Hoyarsabal publishes his *Voyages Avantureux*, the first sailing directions for Newfoundland waters.
c. 1580	Basque whalers employ Innu (Montagnais) in processing oil.
1583	Sir Humfry Gilbert visits St. John's, is provisioned by Portuguese fishermen, claims Newfoundland for Britain, and drowns at Sable Island en route to New England.
1586-1587	John Davis explores the northern Labrador coast.
1588	England defeats the Spanish Armada. From this time West Country fishing crews displace the Portuguese and other European crews from the east coast of Newfoundland.
1597	English attempt to seize the Magdalen Islands' walrus fishery.
1598	Abortive French colony on Sable Island.
By 1605	Mi'kmaq trading with French Basque fishermen at Placentia.
1609	Bretons and Inuit fight a pitched battle at Boutitout near Englee.
1610	John Guy's colony at Cupids, the first English settlement in what is now Canada.
1612	Guy trades with the Beothuk in Trinity Bay.
By 1618	Some of the Cupids colonists resettle at Harbour Grace.
By 1620	St. John's settled.
1620	Richard Whitbourne publishes his best-selling call for colonization, *Discourse and Discovery of Newfoundland*.
1621-1629	Sir George Calvert sponsors the Province of Avalon with a colony at Ferryland.

1626	William Vaughan publishes *The Golden Fleece*, the first book written in Newfoundland—or at least pretends to have been.
1628	Bristol's Hope governor Robert Hayman publishes *Quodlibets*, one of the first works of literature written in North America north of Mexico.
1634	First Western Charter defines the informal administrative role of the "Fishing Admirals."
1638-1651	Sir David Kirke Governor of the Newfoundland Plantation at Ferryland.
1639	Lewis Kirke taxes French Basques fishing in Trinity Bay.
1642-1648	English Civil War between King and Parliament.
1649	Execution of Charles I.
1651-1654	John Treworgie of Maine and other Newfoundland Commissioners attempt to recover Kirke's Newfoundland profits for the revolutionary Commonwealth government.
1653	The Council of State recognizes planters' rights to waterfront property.
1660	Restoration of Charles II.
1661	Second Western Charter encourages Newfoundland settlement by exempting planters from restrictions on transatlantic passage. Proprietorship of Avalon restored to the Calverts...on paper. In fact, the Kirkes continue to dominate the southern Avalon.
1662	The French settle a colony at Plaisance, but the governor and eleven others die in a mutiny.
1665-1667	Second Dutch War. Admiral De Ruyter attacks the English Shore. The house Guy built at Cupids is burned to the ground.
1670-1685	Consolidation of the colony at Plaisance under the governor, Sieur La Poippe.
1671	First French census of habitants in Placentia Bay. Mi'kmaq people are among those reported in the early French censuses. The Western Charter amended to require planters to live at least 6 miles from shore.

1672-1674	Third Dutch War. The Dutch burn parts of St. John's, Ferryland, and other outports.
1675	Captain Sir John Berry, RN, declines to enforce an order to ask the planters to leave Newfoundland and takes the first census of the English Shore.
1676	The second-generation St. John's planter John Downing writes a widely circulated paper on "The Manner of Catching and Making Fish in Newfoundland."
1677	The Council for Trade and Plantations recognizes the Newfoundland planters and orders that they not be disturbed, effectively rescinding the unenforceable 6-mile rule.
c. 1680	Death of merchant Lady Sara Kirke at Ferryland. English planters settle north of Bonavista.
1680s	Open warfare between Breton fishing crews and Inuit bands in the Strait of Belle Isle.
1681	Poor catches blamed on overfishing, lead to a crisis in the fishery. Marine Ordinances of Louis XIV codify traditional practices in the French migratory fishery.
1682	Captain Daniel Jones, RN, attempts to prevent New England ships from carrying fishing servants from St. John's.
1689-1698	King William's War with France.
1689	John Thornton publishes *The English Pilot* with important charts of Newfoundland waters.
1690s	French censuses record habitants in Placentia Bay, the Burin Peninsula, and near Bay d'Espoir.
1694	Louis Jolliet explores the Labrador coast. English planters burn Plaisance.
1696-1697	French and Canadian troops raze the English Shore and deport the planters.
1698	Planters resettle the English Shore. British fortify St. John's. First Anglican Church at St. John's.
1699	King William's Act to Encourage the Trade to Newfoundland defines the property rights of planters.

CHAPTER III

The "Long" Eighteenth Century, 1697-1815

Olaf U. Janzen

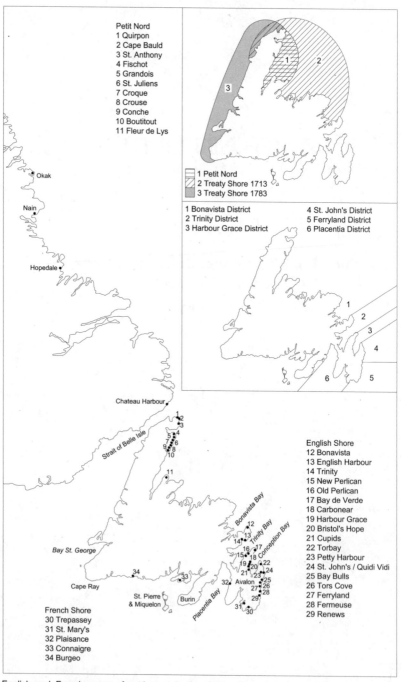

Petit Nord
1 Quirpon
2 Cape Bauld
3 St. Anthony
4 Fischot
5 Grandois
6 St. Juliens
7 Croque
8 Crouse
9 Conche
10 Boutitout
11 Fleur de Lys

1 Petit Nord
2 Treaty Shore 1713
3 Treaty Shore 1783

1 Bonavista District   4 St. John's District
2 Trinity District   5 Ferryland District
3 Harbour Grace District   6 Placentia District

Okak
Nain
Hopedale

Chateau Harbour

Strait of Belle Isle

Bay St. George

Cape Ray

St. Pierre & Miquelon   Burin

French Shore
30 Trepassey
31 St. Mary's
32 Plaisance
33 Connaigre
34 Burgeo

Bonavista Bay
Trinity Bay
Conception Bay
Avalon
Placentia Bay

English Shore
12 Bonavista
13 English Harbour
14 Trinity
15 New Perlican
16 Old Perlican
17 Bay de Verde
18 Carbonear
19 Harbour Grace
20 Bristol's Hope
21 Cupids
22 Torbay
23 Petty Harbour
24 St. John's / Quidi Vidi
25 Bay Bulls
26 Tors Cove
27 Ferryland
28 Fermeuse
29 Renews

English and French areas of settlement in the eighteenth century. Insets indicate the shifting boundaries, and changes in 1783 to the boundaries of the Treaty Shore.

The eighteenth century was extremely significant in the history of Newfoundland and Labrador. Levels of production, employment, and revenue in the British cod fisheries soared, while the French fisheries, once more substantial than those of Great Britain, now fell behind. Indeed, the French were forced off the island of Newfoundland itself, thereby opening the door to the expansion of British settlement beyond the old English Shore. New commercial activities like salmon and seal fisheries developed. The inhabitant population of Newfoundland began to expand steadily in size; by 1815 it exceeded the seasonal migrant fisherman population. This growth disturbed some who still favoured a purely migratory ship fishery. Yet for many, the resident population was a blessing, not a curse. For the West Country merchants, who consolidated their control over the Newfoundland fishery and trade during that century, settlement brought great prosperity. A few merchants even became extremely wealthy and powerful, owning fleets of ships, employing hundreds of fishermen, and dominating the lives of the inhabitants. Ironically, that same prosperity enabled the West Country merchants to shift out of the fisheries and increasingly into trade, particularly when the fishing industry found itself in difficulty, as happened more than once in that century. At the same time, the expansion and diversification in the Newfoundland planter society and economy allowed local merchants to assume a more significant role in the fishery and local trade. In effect, the triumph of the British migratory fishery at Newfoundland during the eighteenth century set the stage for its own extinction.

Of course, no one could have predicted any of this when the eighteenth century began. At the end of the previous century, the French fished on more of the Newfoundland coast than did the British; they fished on the offshore banks which British fishermen ignored (with the possible exception of New England fishermen), and the French fisheries employed more men, more boats, and caught and cured more fish than did the British fisheries. During the recent war (1689-1697) the French had seemingly controlled events in Newfoundland. Operating out of their well-defended colony at Plaisance, French military forces had launched savage attacks against the English settlements, burning homes, storehouses, flakes, and stages, and carrying off hundreds of prisoners; they did so again on at least two more occasions during the next war (1702-1713). Meanwhile, the movement of men, gear, and cargoes of cured fish across the North Atlantic—the life blood of the fisheries—was severely disrupted by enemy privateers and the closure of key markets in Europe. Spain, England's most important market for salt cod, was an enemy during this war, and even much of the Italian market was closed because it was under the control or influence of the Spanish crown. Ironically, the fishery itself experienced record catches as the century began, with some boats taking over 400 quintals in a single season, or double the usual yield. But without uninterrupted trade across the Atlantic and free access to markets, the fishery could not prosper, no matter how abundant the fish. Both the migratory and sedentary fisheries therefore declined significantly.

Nevertheless, despite French military successes in Newfoundland during the war, when peace was restored in 1713 and the Treaty of Utrecht signed, it was England, not France, which now dominated Newfoundland. It was England, not France, which was granted sovereignty over the island; it was France, not England, which now withdrew all its settlers from Newfoundland (except for a few who chose to remain under the British flag). Plaisance, the former French colony, now became Placentia, a British possession; similarly, the islands of St. Pierre and Miquelon became British. France retained only the right to fish (but not to settle) on the coast stretching from Cape Bonavista to Pointe Riche on the western coast of Newfoundland, the so-called "Treaty Shore" or "French Shore." France still retained control over Labrador, a new fishing colony quickly sprang up on Cape Breton Island (to be known as Île Royale, with its centre at Louisbourg), and the fishery on the French Shore remained very productive. Yet the French role in the North Atlantic fishing industry and trade was much more constrained than before, while the British fisheries had an opportunity to expand far beyond the physical and productive limitations of the previous century.

And expand they did, slowly at first to be sure, but irreversibly. Merchants and fishermen began to move into former French areas. A few people, like George Skeffington, had already moved beyond Bonavista during the first decade of the eighteenth century, drawn by the commercial potential of the salmon fishery in the region. Others soon followed, sponsoring settlement in return for trading and fishing commitments. Yet the occupation of former French territories, particularly in Placentia Bay and the South Coast, was not as vigorous as expected, possibly because of a crisis in the inshore cod fishery shortly after 1713. For ten years fishermen experienced disastrously poor catches. In 1720, only 120,000 quintals of fish were shipped to European markets, or roughly half of what had been sent fifty years earlier. Fishing merchants went bankrupt, while many Newfoundland residents were forced to return to England or emigrate to America. Many West Country ports dropped out of the Newfoundland trade entirely. Eventually, however, in the late 1720s, the fishery began to recover, and those English ports that had survived the difficulties of that decade—ports like Dartmouth, Barnstable, Bideford, Poole, Exeter (through its outports of Topsham and Teignmouth), and, to a lesser extent, Bristol, as well as the Channel Islands of Jersey and Guernsey—were now poised for better times. For the next sixty years, their merchants would dominate the Newfoundland fishery and trade. The export of dry salt cod to southern Europe soared to 450,000 quintals by the 1770s.

Some of this recovery was caused by the birth after 1713 of a new English fishery. Until then, English fishermen had ignored the offshore bank fishery, leaving it to the French who had a strong market at home for "wet" or

A "Nursery for Seamen"?

Since the 1500s, government officials valued the fishery not only for the wealth it generated through employment and trade, but also as a strategic asset. As a sea power, England depended upon its navy to defend the realm and maritime trade. This meant having not only powerful warships but also experienced mariners ready at all times to serve in those ships. British officials believed that the fishery was a training ground for potential naval recruits—a "nursery" for seamen (a concept, incidentally, that was shared by the French). Most of the thousands of young men hired every spring to work in the fishery were landsmen with no seafaring skills; by working in the migratory fishery, even for just a season or two, they were transformed into capable seamen—or so government believed. Since most of the fishermen were expected to return home at the end of the fishing season, they became a labour reserve that was available to the state whenever war threatened and it became necessary to mobilize and expand the navy with decisive speed and effect.

The merchant-venturers who invested in the Newfoundland fisheries encouraged this image of a "nursery for seamen" because they could use it to pressure government into providing measures to safeguard their investments—measures like the warships accompanying the fishing fleets to and from Newfoundland. But this did not mean that they were prepared to live up to that image. Historians suggest instead that fishing and other maritime interests did their best to avoid giving their men up to the navy when called upon to do so. As a result, the fishery's reputation as a "nursery for seamen" may have been exaggerated. Still, the image of Newfoundland as a "nursery for seamen" persisted at least until 1815, when the advent of nearly a century of general peace greatly reduced the Royal Navy's persistent appetite for recruits.

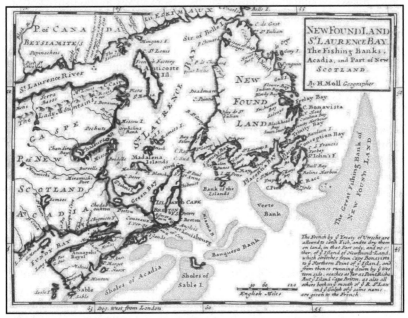

New Found Land, St. Laurence Bay, the fishing banks, Acadia, and part of New Scotland, by H. Moll, geographer, 1713 (courtesy of the Centre for Newfoundland Studies).

"green" cod. The English favoured the inshore fishery which produced high-quality "shore" fish, meaning dried cod or salt cod that was preferred in the Spanish, Portuguese, and Italian markets. The inshore crisis after 1713 forced the British to consider other options. Perhaps by then they had noticed that New England fishermen had fished the offshore banks as early as the 1680s. True, the quality of the fish produced in the bank fishery was inferior—it was commonly called *refuse fish* because it was "refused" by the southern European markets where only the best fish would sell. Yet the New Englanders had no problem selling this lower-grade fish in the less discriminating West Indies market, where the Caribbean sugar economy, with its massive slave-labour force, welcomed cheap food imports, even inferior refuse fish. Moreover, New Englanders by then were regular visitors to Newfoundland, offering North American provisions and forest products in trade for fish. This contact, together with New England willingness to purchase inferior fish, encouraged merchants and residents in Newfoundland to invest in the bank fishery themselves after 1713. By 1770 the English bank fishery was producing 100,000 quintals of fish on top of the nearly 500,000 quintals produced for the European markets.

As it turned out, banking vessels (or simply "bankers") were more productive per man than the boats of the inshore fishery. They required smaller crews and were relatively cheap to build. Such cost advantages helped compensate for the lower price fetched by bank fish. It also made it easier for Newfoundland planters themselves to invest in the fishery. Soon, a significant proportion of the bank fishery was based in Newfoundland, a trend that represents one of the fishery's first major commitments of capital in Newfoundland. In turn, this encouraged people to settle on the island.

The bank fishery also encouraged a new kind of migration to Newfoundland. The smaller crews of the bankers meant that those that still came from Great Britain had room for extra passengers. The fees charged for carrying passengers and their supplies and provisions across the Atlantic covered much of a banker's annual operating costs. Indeed, it is reasonable to assume that in hard times, the passage-money earned by transporting sixty or seventy fishermen and their supplies might well have spelled the difference between an unprofitable voyage and a profitable one. Not surprisingly, a symbiotic relationship developed between the bank fishery, which welcomed passengers, and the migratory bye-boat fishery, whose boat owners needed crews but lacked ships of their own to transport them.

The rise of the bank fishery and the expansion of the passenger trade were just two of several factors that contributed to a remarkable change in Newfoundland's settled population. For decades before 1730, the number of permanent inhabitants in British Newfoundland had fluctuated within a narrow range of roughly 1,000 to 2,000 inhabitants, and was confined to the traditional English Shore. By 1730, the number was closer to 3,000.

Seasonal Round

The inhabitants of Newfoundland had always depended on merchant credit to support themselves, exchanging the promise of fish not yet caught for provisions and supplies. Credit, however, could lead to debt, and, early on, inhabitants learned to supplement both their income and their needs by hunting, gardening, berry-picking, and so on. Over the course of a year, therefore, the inhabitants developed a "seasonal round" of activities necessary to survive in Newfoundland.

In the spring, the fishing fleets arrived with large numbers of seasonal workers as well as all-important supplies like flour, hard bread, salt beef and pork, bacon, and gear which inhabitants purchased against promises of the fish to be caught and cured by fall. Those near salmon rivers and the few fortunate enough to live where seals (valued in the eighteenth century primarily for "train" or oil, not pelts) migrated along the coast used traps and nets to add those resources to their larder and to the inventory of what they delivered to merchants. Capelin made their welcome appearance in late spring and early summer, and gardens were planted, to be tended by women and children; the men made ready for the intense and exhausting inshore cod-fishing season. The summer was devoted entirely to the cod, but by September, the season's catch had been cured and turned over to the merchants. As the fishing fleets departed, attention among the residents would shift to preparations for winter. They harvested whatever their garden plots might yield, ventured out to gather berries, and prepared their homes for the harsh winter to come. On the northeast coast seals might be netted on their return migration.

By late fall, the residents of many communities began to break up into small family units and disperse into the shelter of the woods where they settled into simple shacks for the winter. This practice was known as "winterhousing." A missionary at Trinity in 1764 explained, unnecessarily perhaps, that "The Rich ... go to England" while "The rest that Stay Dissipate through the Woods for subsistence on Venison, hunting, and for getting fire, and Building Boats with their servants." Only a few people, mostly men, remained in Trinity to maintain the fishing premises. Winterhousing was most likely to occur in areas where the forests would support the sort of activities described. It was least likely to occur where shipbuilding, carpentry, and other activities could provide employment that enabled a resident population to support itself through the winter months. Thus, winterhousing was quite prevalent in Trinity and Bonavista Bays, and almost non-existent in the Avalon Peninsula south of St. John's and Placentia.

Finally, as another spring began, the residents made ready for another fishing season.

Thereafter, the resident population of Newfoundland began to expand—to over 5,000 inhabitants in 1765, possibly 10,000 people by the mid-1780s, and nearly 40,000 by 1815. Perhaps more to the point, by 1780 the permanent population exceeded the seasonal migratory population.

What had removed the limitations that had seemingly restrained the size of the permanent population for so many decades before 1730? We know that the number of inhabitants in Newfoundland at the beginning of the eighteenth century, combined with the seasonal influx of several thousand migratory fishermen from England and increasingly from Ireland, had satisfied the needs of the West Country merchants for people to catch and to cure the fish they exported to Europe. The merchants did not really oppose permanent inhabitancy because they needed residents to support their operations and their trade in Newfoundland from one year to the next. The merchants therefore extended credit willingly to the residents in exchange for their salt cod. But by the eighteenth century, more and more merchants concentrated not only on the fishery but also on freighting goods, transporting people, and providing various services in Newfoundland. Whether they transported labour or general cargoes, it is obvious from their cargoes that "fishing ships" were carrying supplies for more than the merchants' own fishing crews. Poole merchants, with substantial interests in Trinity and Bonavista Bays, took the lead in this trend, but others quickly followed. In effect, fishing ships were increasingly functioning as trading ships.

Soon, merchants not only accepted permanent settlement, they encouraged it. Each settler was another customer to supply. This process was already apparent in the seventeenth century, when merchants began transforming "their" fishing rooms into extensive and permanent properties to support their operations. This also weakened loyalty to the practice of allocating fishing rooms on a "first come, first served" basis, because increasingly they were occupied by the crews and servants of West Country fishing merchants throughout the year. Ownership was becoming accepted, and property was routinely passed on to heirs when an owner died. The growing emphasis on the supply trade reinforced this trend. No longer were investors exclusively "fishing merchants." They had become suppliers, shippers, wholesalers, and retailers and, in addition to fishing premises, they now maintained permanent warehouses, wholesale outlets, and trading facilities. To manage these operations, merchants sent junior members of their families to live in Newfoundland. Although not planters in the true sense, many remained in Newfoundland for years, learning the trade, and frequently assuming various administrative responsibilities. And as merchant premises became more permanent, the growth of the resident population accelerated.

Other factors contributed to the increasing number of permanent inhabitants. Other resources became commercially significant. Salmon production rose from an average of 1,000 tierces in the late 1730s to 2,000 per year in the 1760s and 3,000 by the mid-1770s. Inhabitants supplemented their diet and income with fur trapping and sealing. Such activities never replaced the cod fishery yet they were significant, because both were winter activities that complemented the summer cod fishery rather than competed with it for the time and energy of the inhabitant. All produced commodities that could be sold in England.

Gardening also played a role in supporting population growth. Official reports show that the quantity of "improved" land increased steadily through the century, enhancing the ability of residents to feed themselves. Thus, there were 200 hectares of cleared cultivated land and about 300 cattle, 200 sheep, and 300 swine in Conception Bay by 1741. The introduction of the potato by the 1740s gave special significance to those plots, because potatoes gave inhabitants a new and nutritious food that was easy to grow, and may therefore have been a critical factor in accelerating population growth after mid-century.

While alternative resources like salmon, seal, furs, and home-grown vegetables enhanced the ability of people to live in Newfoundland year-round, it must be said that growth of the permanent population was closely related to the continued growth and diversification of the fisheries and trading opportunities at Newfoundland. When the fishery prospered, outfitters would increase production, which meant increasing the size of their seasonal labour force. In turn, seasonal workers who chose to remain in Newfoundland at the end of the season rather than return to Great Britain added to the permanent population. The fact remains that the sedentary and seasonal populations were closely related and the main dynamic in the growth of inhabitancy was the fishery.

Economic and social connections between Newfoundland and other parts of the North Atlantic region were also important in transforming a predominantly migratory fishery into an increasingly residential one. One such connection, with the Anglo-American colonies of mainland North America, has already been mentioned. Another was the expanding role of Ireland as a source of labour and provisions for the fisheries. Both connections left an indelible mark on the character of eighteenth-century Newfoundland.

Anglo-American Connections

American vessels came to Newfoundland both as a destination for products that they could sell and as a place where they could acquire fish for re-sale elsewhere. American trading vessels also encouraged a migration out of Newfoundland to mainland North America. New England had developed its own fishery in the seventeenth century. Although they were already competing with the Newfoundland fisheries for a share of the European salt cod market by 1660, the Caribbean market quickly became more important to New England merchants than those in Europe. But New Englanders also came to Newfoundland to trade. By the 1740s New Englanders were purchasing fish in exchange for foodstuffs and supplies that were cheaper and better in quality than those from Great Britain—flour, bread, and livestock from the American colonies, molasses and rum from the West Indies, and non-edibles like tobacco, building lumber, barrel staves, and marine supplies like pitch, tar, turpentine, masts, and spars, also from the American colonies. In 1715, forty-two Anglo-American vessels were reported at Newfoundland; by 1774 there were 175. Some who came to trade would stay permanently, and even became quite prominent in local Newfoundland society. Michael Gill, who became the Judge of the Vice-Admiralty Court in 1751, was a New

What Do We Mean by "Permanent Inhabitants"?

Permanent residents or "planters" had become a fixture on the island by the eighteenth century. A planter was someone who owned a "plantation" or "fishing room" and at least one shallop. Often a planter employed others (usually men) to work for him (or her; there were some "mistresses" who owned boat fishing operations), typically for two summers and one winter. Once their contract was over, servants were expected to return to Great Britain. The planter bought supplies from the fishing ships and, by the eighteenth century, from merchants who maintained increasingly complex commercial facilities in Newfoundland for the purpose. The planter then agreed to turn over a portion of the season's catch. The servants were paid out of whatever was left.

Some planters were descendants of seventeenth-century colonists. Others were fishermen who chose to remain in Newfoundland when their contract expired rather than return to England or Ireland. For some, Newfoundland offered a degree of personal success that eluded them back home. For others, the frequent wars of the eighteenth century made it more difficult to return to Europe (because diminishing shipping volumes and rising insurance rates in wartime caused passenger rates to increase), or less attractive (because war brought an increased risk at home of having to serve in the navy; see Sidebar, "Nursery for Seamen"). Whatever the reason for remaining permanently in Newfoundland, everyone depended upon the fishery for survival. Some planters prospered, owning as many as five boats and thirty or so servants. But most were one- or two-boat operations. Supplies bought on credit against the unpredictable outcome of the season's fishery were expensive, to cover the cost of the supplier's risks. This made planters susceptible to a growing debt load, though life in Newfoundland was probably no worse than life in England or Ireland at that time. A few eventually returned to Great Britain to shift into another occupation. Some found life too difficult and headed off to America.

All this meant that the composition and character of the "population" of Newfoundland changed continuously, ebbing and flowing like the tide. In the summer, most of the people were really "seasonal" workers who had arrived in the spring and returned to England or Ireland in the fall. Some were "temporary" residents who remained in Newfoundland for a few years, eventually to return to the Old Country. Only a few were true "permanent" inhabitants, people who never left, but had families and whose children were born and raised in Newfoundland. We must therefore not take "official" population figures at face value, because they often blurred the distinctions between temporary and truly permanent residents. When the century began, the permanent population hovered between 1,000 and 2,000 people. What made the eighteenth century unusual was that something happened after the 1720s to cause the population to begin to expand in numbers, slowly at first, but irresistibly. Historians are still trying to puzzle out the factors that caused the permanent population to grow in this way.

Englander, as was William Keen, who became the Naval Officer at St. John's and later a magistrate.

Some British merchants complained about the growing number of Americans; they begrudged every fish that went in trade without passing first through their own hands. In turn, British officials were sympathetic to the complaints, because the Americans were also accused of smuggling and of encouraging fishermen to abandon their labour contracts and migrate instead to mainland North America. Yet residential and seasonal fishermen alike needed American provisions and supplies. More to the point, many West Country merchants accepted the American trade by mid-century. They understood that England could no longer supply commodities like bread and flour to Newfoundland in the quantities needed. They also recognized that the trade to Newfoundland from the British Isles on the one hand and from the American colonies on the other were complementary, not competitive. England was increasingly the source of hardware and dry goods such as fishing gear and clothing; the American colonies provided cereal products, livestock, lumber, and rum. Diversity in the source of imports to Newfoundland was particularly beneficial to the inhabitants because it meant that, in contrast to the French, they were less likely to be cut off from essentials like provisions whenever the outbreak of a war caused disruptions to transatlantic trade.

The Irish Connection

If the American colonies were one important element in nurturing the fishery and inhabitants of Newfoundland, Ireland was another. But to understand how and why Ireland became so important to Newfoundland, we must first recognize that most migration to Newfoundland before the eighteenth century, whether seasonal or permanent, had been predominantly English, specifically from Devonshire and Dorset in the West Country. The merchant was central to this process, recruiting labourers and passengers during the winter and early spring, then transporting them to Newfoundland. As merchants broadened their activity to include not only support for the fishery but also trade with the residents, their increasingly elaborate commercial premises in Newfoundland nurtured settlement growth because residents could now rely confidently on those premises for supplies and credit to endure the harsh winter months. These same processes brought the Irish to Newfoundland.

There were Irish in Newfoundland in the 1500s but the link between Ireland and Newfoundland became significant largely because of the West Country merchants. By the late 1600s, West Country ships and vessels making their way to Newfoundland had begun stopping at seaports like Waterford and Cork in southeastern Ireland to stock up on salt beef, pork, butter, and biscuit, which were all more abundant and cheaper than English "wet" provisions. Soon they also began taking on Irish labour. The Irish were usually farm labourers from the hinterland behind the Irish ports—Waterford county, southwest Wexford, southern Kilkenny, southeastern Tipperary, and southeastern Cork. As landsmen, they were inexperienced (hence "green" men or "youngsters") and therefore cheaper to hire than West Country men. At first, the flow of Irishmen to Newfoundland was relatively insignificant. But it accelerated in the 1720s and 1730s. Perhaps the collapse of the inshore fishery after 1713 discouraged West Country recruits from going to Newfoundland. Perhaps

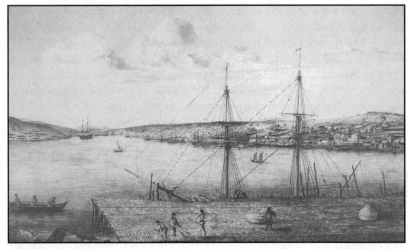

Watercolour, [Nicholas Pocock?] "View of the Upper End of the Harbour from a Little Below Fort William," St. John's, Newfoundland, c. late eighteenth century (courtesy of Library and Archives Canada, No. 1996-381).

the birth of the bank fishery contributed to this trend because it required fewer skills than the inshore fishery. The expansion into former French areas beyond Trepassey and St. Mary's into Placentia Bay may also have reinforced these patterns.

Conditions in Ireland also encouraged Irish migration. Crop failures in the countryside and unemployment in the towns were not uncommon and contributed to an economic uncertainty that stood in contrast to the apparent prosperity of the Newfoundland fishery. And since it was so easy to hire onto a fishing ship that had stopped at Ireland for provisions, Newfoundland became an obvious solution to local economic dilemmas. By the 1730s, 1,000 Irish passengers were being carried to Newfoundland annually; by the 1770s and 1780s, 5,000 Irish came to Newfoundland each year. Many would stay permanently—by 1750 the Irish made up 25 per cent of the population, and by 1800 half the population was of Irish descent.

Implications of an Expanding Population

These several interrelated trends—the growing permanence of the commercial establishments, the diversification of Newfoundland's commercial linkages with other parts of the North Atlantic rim, the ensuing expansion in migratory labour force, and, closely linked, the expanding population of permanent inhabitants, as well as the ethnic character of the population—all shaped Newfoundland's transformation in the eighteenth century from a fishery to a settled society. These trends also came with several important implications and challenges.

The most obvious implication was the need for an administrative structure better suited to a permanently rooted, increasingly complex, expanding population. King William's Act of 1699 had been a set of trade regulations, not a legal framework for administering a permanent society. It had codified and summarized the customs and practices of the fishery and trade, and continued to provide the basis for regulating the fishery for the next seventy-five years. The Act did *not* recognize Newfoundland as a colony, though it *did* concede and give effective recognition to the existence of settlement. King William's Act most certainly did *not* prohibit settlement, though it did constrain it to a degree. By then, the British government had also initiated the practice of assigning a small number of warships to the Newfoundland "station." They escorted the fishing and trading vessels to Newfoundland every spring, and remained there until the fall when they escorted the fleets back, either to Great Britain or (in the case of those ships carrying fish to market) southern Europe. The warships patrolled the coast and occasionally the fishing banks, watching for anything that might interfere or threaten the fishery, such as over-enthusiastic French warships patrolling their own fishing fleets, or pirates (which briefly became a problem in the 1720s).

The actual task of attending to disputes within the fishery was, however, assigned to the fishery itself. The Act recognized the system of "fishing admirals" which had emerged over a century earlier. Yet, as the choicer harbours developed substantial resident populations and as disputes began to arise that were less directly related to the fishery itself, the weakness of this rudimentary system of administration became apparent. Few fishing admirals relished the distraction and responsibility of maintaining civil order: they were there to fish, not to administer the law. Besides, the fishing admirals were present only during the fishing season; no one was in charge once the fishing fleet headed home. Yet it was during the winter that problems like assault, theft, murder, or even riots that we associate with poverty, alcoholism, destitution, and religious tensions became most serious.

King William's Act did allow the right to appeal decisions to the commander of the naval escort which convoyed the fishing fleet to Newfoundland each year. Those commanders therefore found themselves assuming a growing measure of responsibility for administering the Act. Therein lay the seeds of the system of naval governors. As early as 1708, an Order-in-Council placed naval commodores in overall charge of the fishery. Even so, the basic problem remained: like the fishing admirals, the naval officers were present for only a few months of the year, so that there was no one empowered to maintain law and order once the fishing fleets and warships departed in the fall. A more systematic and permanent approach to maintaining peace and order in Newfoundland was needed.

The British authorities therefore began to establish an ever more elaborate judicial and administrative framework. This was done gradually, reluctantly, and never as part of some larger, coherent plan. Instead, government took existing customs and local practices, added statutory regulations, and placed this emerging system of governance under the supervision of the naval officers stationed each season in the fishery. In 1729, the British government began instructing one of the naval officers serving with the annual convoy to exercise the civil authority of governor, including the power to appoint civilians. The first governor appointed under this new system, Captain Henry Osborne, promptly divided the English Shore into six judicial districts, appointing magistrates to each one. He also arranged for the construction of a court house, jail, and stocks. But Osborne was careful to place limits on the powers of these magistrates: they were not supposed to infringe on the civil authority of the fishing admirals, and cases involving capital crimes (crimes punishable by death) were still to be tried in England. Some people still complained that the innovations would lead to further regulation and interference in the fishery. But their practical benefits were quickly recognized, and it soon became apparent that the people best suited to serve as magistrates by virtue of having the necessary education, influence, and time for the job were the merchants themselves or their agents. The governors, who were generally appointed for only a year or two and were never at Newfoundland for more than a few months, relied heavily upon local merchants for advice and assistance. Hostility therefore gave way to acceptance as merchants realized that the new judicial system would be in their control. Soon the magistrates were an accepted fixture in Newfoundland.

Over time, the naval governors introduced additional measures to make the system of administration more effective. Thus, in 1741 Governor Smith appointed William Keen as Naval Officer at St. John's, a civilian position to monitor incoming and out-going vessels at St. John's and collect fees from them. In 1750 Governor Rodney supervised the establishment of a permanent Court of Oyer and Terminer to hear cases involving capital crimes, followed in 1751 by a Vice-Admiralty Court at St. John's responsible for enforcing trade laws.

Newfoundland's emerging legal and administrative system was by no means perfect. The magistrates were unpaid, as was the case in England and elsewhere in British America, and therefore relied on licensing fees and fines to cover their expenses; this led to abuses. And since many magistrates were prominent members of the community, the justice they dispensed was often biased in favour of friends, relatives, and business associates, or more generally against people at the lower levels of the social and economic system. Yet this was offset by the adoption of the system of "governor's surrogates," in which the naval governor delegated his authority to subordinate naval officers stationed in the fishery. Consistent with the appeal procedure defined by King William's Act, this allowed anyone who felt that a fishing admiral or magistrate had ruled unfairly in a case to appeal to the governor through the commanding officer of whatever warship happened to be patrolling in that area. The result was a system of government with the flexibility to adjust to a rapidly changing social environment.

Government tolerated, even encouraged, administrative innovations like these because the residents seemed at times to be especially turbulent. The Irish, ironically, were often blamed for that turbulence—ironic because the Irish were there in the first place because the fishery needed them, and continued to be brought to Newfoundland in large numbers by West Country fishing interests. Yet those same fishing interests, the planters, and many of the naval officers became alarmed by the growing numbers of Irish residents, who soon made up the majority of Newfoundland's winter population. Concern had been expressed as early as 1720, and it became common to accuse the Irish of lawlessness (especially during the hard winters), to which would be added predictions of treason, even revolt, whenever England found herself at war with her Catholic rivals, France and Spain. Occasionally sensational events, like the murder in 1754 of planter and magistrate William Keen by a group of nine Irish men and one Irish woman, caused animosity against the Irish to become particularly vehement. Another notorious incident was the enthusiasm with which Irishmen helped the French plunder St. John's in 1762—the Church of England minister reported that "the People are almost all ruined." Such attitudes must, however, be placed in context. Anti-Irish and anti-Catholic bigotry was widespread in the eighteenth-century British Empire and it would have been surprising had such feelings not been evident in Newfoundland. We must not forget that many Irish living permanently in Newfoundland were themselves planters and property-owners, even merchants, and were as concerned by winter lawlessness as their English counterparts, even if they did not have the same civil rights. The problem was that, when times were hard in the fishery, many servants were left unpaid and abandoned by their masters, and turned to crime as their only means of survival. That more of the Irish were servants meant that criminal behaviour tended easily to be associated with the Irish, and English prejudices were in turn reinforced.

If, therefore, civil unrest and lawlessness contributed to the development of a legal and administrative framework, there was also recognition that the expanding population created social and economic conditions that needed to be addressed. Normally, in most eighteenth-century societies, such responsibilities and work were left to organized religion. Religious institutions provided society with moral guidance and leadership, education, and training. In Newfoundland, like everything else, this was complicated by the migratory character of the fishery. It was assumed that the spiritual and moral needs of the fishermen were satisfied by churches and clergymen in England, either before the men left for Newfoundland or after their return. Clergymen in Newfoundland were unnecessary for a transient labour force. After all, the most obvious functions of any clergy are to provide the sacraments of baptism, marriage, death, and so on, none of which were relevant to a migratory fishery except perhaps accidental death. The growth of a permanent population, with accompanying social tensions, changed this attitude, particularly since a substantial proportion of that growing population was Irish Catholic at a time when the practice of Catholicism was forbidden in Newfoundland.

The earliest clergy and preachers to appear regularly in eighteenth-century Newfoundland belonged to the Church of England and were sponsored by the Society for the Propagation of the Gospel in Foreign Parts (SPG). The SPG had been established in 1701 as a privately financed organization dedicated to service as the missionary arm of the Church of England. It sent clergy to colonial outposts throughout the empire. All Church of England clergy in Newfoundland before 1775 were SPG missionaries; all schoolmasters were supported by the SPG.

The organization and the activities of the SPG met with the full approval and support of the British government. It is necessary to remember that religion at this time was regarded as a powerful force for maintaining order, particularly among the poorer, uneducated inhabitants. Other Protestant dominations were tolerated in overseas territories, but they were always suspected of encouraging values which were incompatible with the values of order, hierarchy, and obedience favoured by the authorities. Consequently, the authorities welcomed the efforts of the SPG to minister to the religious needs of Newfoundland. The earliest clergyman to receive SPG support there was John Jackson, who had established himself permanently at St. John's in 1701, the same year that the SPG was established. Other settlements gradually acquired SPG clergy—Bonavista in the 1720s, Trinity around 1730, Harbour Grace in 1765—thus firmly identifying those settlements as being in the forefront of an emerging society. SPG clergymen often served outside the pulpit as magistrates as well as teachers for the first schools.

Yet the SPG had mixed success in Newfoundland. The expectations of their missionaries were often too high. They refused to compromise with other religions, particularly Catholics, and they were too few in number to meet the religious needs of every community. Part of the problem, of course, was the dispersed nature of the population along hundreds of kilometres of coastline. Apart from regional centres like St. John's, Placentia, Harbour Grace, and Trinity, settlements were tiny and lacked effective means of communications except by sea. Each settlement was an outport of a regional centre, from which came the essential provisions, gear, and supplies required by the fishery, and through which the season's catch would be sent to market. The regional centres in turn interacted directly with an English West Country home port, not with each other. A sense of belonging to a common society existed at best within a bay but not throughout the island, at least not during the eighteenth century. This fragmentation might have been overcome by the social and spiritual services of the clergy, but their small numbers meant that only the largest centres received such attention. Less fortunate communities made do with the services of naval chaplains serving in visiting warships. Thus, when HMS *Panther* stopped at Placentia in 1772, its chaplain was called upon to baptize forty-two children in one day.

The inability of the SPG to satisfy every spiritual and social need contributed to the willingness of dissenting clergy and evangelical preachers to fill the gap, though they too tended to appear in centres large

Sketch of the Island of Newfoundland done from the latest observations, by James Cook, 1763 (Centre for Newfoundland Studies).

enough to provide a following capable of supporting them. In the 1770s and 1780s we see Methodist, Congregationalist, and even lay preachers—men like Laurence Coughlan, John Hopkins, and John Jones—preaching to receptive groups in St. John's and Conception Bay. But their emphasis on personal revelation, religious enthusiasm, and high moral tone disturbed those who viewed religion as an instrument of social control, while teachings that stressed freedom of the will were regarded as threats by those who expected the clergy to serve as agents for promoting order among the poorer, uneducated inhabitants. Lacking the sanction of the Church of England, dissenting clergy faced opposition from the authorities and local merchants alike.

The role of religion as an instrument of social order helps explain the shift in official attitudes towards Roman Catholicism. For much of the eighteenth century, Catholics faced severe discrimination in Newfoundland. In part this was a legacy of England's long and often violent history of anti-Catholicism; indeed, discrimination against Catholics was official British policy everywhere—Catholics were barred from holding public office in the British Empire, and in Newfoundland, and governors' instructions routinely stipulated that the "free exercise of Religion" was to be granted to all persons "except Papists." Anti-Catholic feeling on the island was complicated by the fact that, with few exceptions, all Catholics were also Irish. Anti-Catholic feeling was often impossible to separate from anti-Irish hostility. Yet instances of open repression were the exception rather than the rule. Generally, the

A dancing woman, drawing by Shawnadithit, c. 1828 (courtesy of The Rooms Provincial Museum).

Mary March (Demasduit), sketched by Lady Henrietta Martha Hamilton, 1819 (Library and Archives Canada).

Beothuk

The Beothuk were the descendants of the Recent Indians that came to Newfoundland 2,000 years ago. We refer to their pre-European contact culture as "Little Passage." Little Passage archaeological sites contain no European material culture. Sites inhabited by the Beothuk immediately following contact with Europeans contain materials of European manufacture that are almost always modified into traditional tools, for example, iron nails from unoccupied European fishing places were flattened into projectile points.

The extinction of the Beothuk tribe has haunted Newfoundlanders to this day, and it is often asserted that it was they who were responsible. In fact, the reasons for the extinction are complex. Unlike the Mi'kmaq and the Inuit, for instance, the Beothuk decided not to engage directly with European settlers and visitors. No fur trade developed here as on the mainland. Instead, the Beothuk chose to keep themselves to themselves.

At the same time, Europeans began to encroach upon Beothuk territory. Their occupation of the coast threatened Beothuk access to marine resources, and exposed them to diseases against which the Beothuk had no immunity. Similarly, the increasing Mi'kmaq presence in Newfoundland during the eighteenth century may have reduced Beothuk access to caribou and other resources of the interior. The Beothuk reacted by harassing Europeans, who in turn went after the Beothuk. The result was sporadic violence along the northeast coast. Well-meaning, if belated and clumsy, attempts by the Newfoundland authorities as early as the 1760s and again in 1811, as well as by members of the "Boeothick Institution," to establish friendly relations with the Beothuk, failed. Mutual mistrust and suspicion were too firmly entrenched.

The last known Beothuk, Shawnadithit, died of tuberculosis in St. John's on 6 June 1829.

population was too dispersed for religious antagonisms to become active beyond the local level, while the absence of a vigorous Established Church provided no champion for anti-Catholic feeling. Most importantly, the Irish were there because the fishing interests, including the planters, wanted them there. Consequently, freedom of worship was extended to the Catholics in 1779 and, in 1784, the first officially sanctioned priest arrived at St. John's. Proof that Catholicism could be as useful as the Church of England in preserving public order came in 1800, when Catholic Bishop James O'Donel exposed a conspiracy within the military garrison at St. John's (amongst the Irish troops, of course, but also including a number of civilians) to rise up, murder the people of property (who were invariably English), and loot the town before escaping to the United States.

"Esquimaux Indians of the Coast of Labrador" communicated by a Moravian missionary, drawn by Garret, engraved by Chapman, published by C. Jones, 17 October 1818 (from Charles de Volpi, *Newfoundland: A Pictorial Record*).

Reference to the military garrison points to another reason why the English in Newfoundland were suspicious of Catholics. For much of the time between 1689 and 1815, England was at war with Catholic France, its neighbour and chief North Atlantic rival. The vicious Winter War of 1696-1697 had prompted the British government to establish a permanent garrison in Newfoundland for the first time ever, despite the

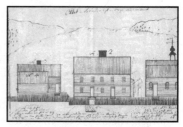

Reproduction of a pencil drawing of the mission buildings at Okak, Labrador, c. 1781. The buildings are numbered two through four and explanations as to their function and physical dimensions are given at the bottom of the drawing (Archives and Manuscripts, Memorial University Library).

persistent belief that the defence of the fishery was better served through the exercise of sea power than by fortifications. As the British Secretary of State explained in 1766, Newfoundland was best defended by warships, and fortifications were useful only to provide a refuge for "protecting the Vessels, Seamen and fishing Utensils from a sudden Attack." He added that "the protection of the Inhabitants settled on the Island is neither practicable nor desirable." Nevertheless, England and France both held the economic value of fishery in the highest regard, and, time and again, Newfoundland was caught in the cross-fire when the two powers went to war. Great Britain therefore did construct military installations in Newfoundland. For the most part, these were concentrated in St. John's and, to a lesser extent, Placentia. Yet when France went to war with England in 1778 and again in 1793, the British government responded to appeals from several other communities for protective measures by installing gun batteries as harbour defences.

Military measures for its defence inadvertently contributed to Newfoundland's continuing growth and diversification. Considerable money was poured into building the fortifications at St. John's and Placentia; more was pumped into the local economy by the small garrisons installed on the island. Military personnel became consumers of local goods and services, while garrison pay chests occasionally injected hard currency into the economy, especially St. John's, where it enhanced the town's emerging importance as Newfoundland's administrative, strategic, and economic hub. The construction and repair of the garrison fortifications provided employment, encouraged the appearance of specialty skills and trades, and stimulated local agriculture. The military garrisons not only included wives and children of the soldiers, they also attracted domestic servants, skilled labourers, tradesmen, and artisans. The military presence even added pomp and ceremony to the social life of the community. In short, military garrisons strongly influenced the development of the communities in which they were stationed.

The wars with France helped redefine Newfoundland itself. With the Treaty of Utrecht, France gave up the territories it had occupied and settled and was left with only the right to fish on the French Shore. When the Seven Years War drew to a close in 1763, France lost the rest of its North American empire (except for St. Pierre and Miquelon, which were now returned to France). The loss of so much territory added considerably to the importance of what little was left, and the French not only became more defensive about their fishing rights in Newfoundland, but also more assertive in defining where those rights applied. It was partly for this reason that the British authorized a series of hydrographic surveys. British scientific knowledge of Newfoundland geography was very weak, but nowhere was this more the case than on the Labrador coast, which had formerly belonged to France, or on the south coast and the west coast, where British fishermen had established only a superficial presence. James Cook, who had demonstrated his talent for hydrography during the war, was appointed to the task. Labrador also presented the British with an opportunity to establish there what increasingly no longer existed in Newfoundland—a purely migratory fishery. For this reason, Labrador was attached to the administration of Newfoundland, and Hugh Palliser, the naval commodore and civil governor from 1764 to 1768, now dedicated himself to restoring a vigorous migratory fishery.

This, however, was easier said than done. Friction between the Inuit and fishermen threatened plans to encourage the fishery on the Labrador

A view looking southeast to Placentia, by J.S. Meres. Castle Hill is situated to the far right with Jerseyside just below Placentia, logbook of HMS *Pegasus*, 1786 (courtesy of Library and Archives Canada).

coast. Governor Palliser therefore encouraged the "Unitas Fratrum," better known as the Moravians, to establish a mission far to the north of the areas frequented by European fishermen in hopes that such a mission would cause the Inuit to lose interest in travelling south for trade—and violent encounters—with the fishermen. The Moravians established their first mission at Nain in 1771, another at Okak in 1776, and still another at Hopedale in 1782. These missions seemed to have the effect desired by Palliser. Conflict between Inuit and fishermen fell off, although not perhaps as quickly as he would have liked.

It was also during this period that Palliser directed an expedition into the Exploits River Valley to make contact with the elusive Beothuk people, in hopes of establishing amicable relations and bringing an end to clashes between native people and fishermen on the northeast coast. The expedition, led by Lieutenant John Cartwright, failed to make any contact. Meanwhile, on the south coast, Royal Navy warships were discouraging large family groups of Nova Scotia Mi'kmaq from visiting St. Pierre, which by then was the only centre of French Catholicism in the region. Rebuffed by both the British and the French, the Mi'kmaq headed instead to the west coast where they settled in Bay St. George. In his dealings with the Beothuk and the Mi'kmaq in Newfoundland, and with the Inuit in Labrador, Palliser was driven by a belief that the fisheries should remain a predominantly seasonal activity. By establishing peaceful contact with native people, or discouraging their arrival from elsewhere, he hoped to foster a peaceful and harmonious environment in which the fishery could thrive. Yet Palliser's expectations were no longer realistic. The growth of a settled society in Newfoundland and even in Labrador, with all the complexities that entailed, was becoming irreversible.

From Fishery to Colony

When the French swept through the English Shore during the wars of 1689-1697 and 1702-1713, destroying almost everything in their paths, the suffering of the inhabitants had been horrific, yet the fishery had quickly recovered—as severe as the damage was, the fishery could survive such destruction because it had not yet invested in, or become dependent upon, permanent facilities on the island. This was no longer the case by mid-century. By then, the fishery and trade both depended on extensive storage, service, and trading establishments in many harbours. Whenever war caused the British migratory fishery to contract, the growing residential population could take up much of the slack. This did not mean that the fishery could maintain peacetime production levels in times of war, but it did mean that the British never stopped producing fish at Newfoundland, not even in wartime. In contrast, the French fishery in the eighteenth century was increasingly a migratory one, subject to complete interruption with every war. The only residential fishery left to the French after 1763 was that of St. Pierre and Miquelon, and the British quickly captured these islands whenever war with France broke out. And with every interruption to its fishery and trade, the French share of the European market diminished while the British share increased. The worst setback came after 1793, when war suspended the French fishery, not just for a few years but for an entire generation. By the time a lasting peace was restored in 1815, the French could not recover all the ground they had lost.

The wars that brought the eighteenth century to a close had a profound effect not only on the French fisheries but on Newfoundland itself, completing its transformation from a seasonal fishery to a settled colony in all but administrative fact. The British migratory fishery at Newfoundland had already been traumatized by a massive production of fish in 1788—more fish than the markets in Europe could absorb. Prices had collapsed and a series of bankruptcies rippled through the trade. The bankruptcies in turn brought on something of a crisis in the Newfoundland judiciary which had difficulty coping with all the legal fallout. Some significant reforms were therefore introduced with the creation by Parliament of a Court of Civil Jurisdiction in 1791, followed the next year by a "Supreme Court of Judicature of the Island of Newfoundland," headed by John Reeves as the Chief Justice. A system of surrogate courts was established in the outports. Though they had to be renewed each year by Parliament, these measures eventually became a permanent fixture.

The wars of 1793 to 1815 brought clear indications that what had once been a predominantly migratory activity was now becoming a predominantly residential one. One such sign was the rapid increase in the permanent population by some 300 per cent between 1785 and 1815. More and more migratory servants chose to remain in Newfoundland rather than return to

England. This may be explained by the elimination of England's rivals in the fish trade, giving the British a virtual monopoly in the European markets. The harsh aftermath of the market glut of 1788 therefore gave way to such an improvement of conditions that, by 1807, fishermen were even able to settle their accounts with the merchants. Such economic buoyancy must have encouraged many to settle in Newfoundland.

The unprecedented prosperity certainly contributed to the escalation of immigration into Newfoundland. Although immigration would not hit its peak until after 1815, the final decade of the Napoleonic Wars clearly marks the beginning of this massive flow of people. Many immigrants still came from the English West Country, but most of the new arrivals between 1803 and 1836 were Irish. Yet immigration was not the only growth factor. Natural increase was also substantial, a fact which would not have been possible had there not been a significant increase in the number of women on the island by the late eighteenth century. Indeed, some have argued that nothing defined the growing permanence of the Newfoundland population more than the growing proportion of women and children. Although the number of unattached males still exceeded the number of women, the imbalance in the ratio of the sexes was not nearly as great as it had been when the century began. By the early 1800s, the number of women had risen sufficiently to allow the English population in Newfoundland to keep pace with the growing tide of Irish immigration.

Nowhere was the impact of that growth felt more acutely than in St. John's. There, the speed and scale of population growth intensified a number of problems normally associated with urban colonial society such as overcrowding, a lack of sanitary services, and the absence of social institutions such as police, hospitals, and schools through which public welfare and order could be preserved. Some efforts were made at social and cultural improvement— the Benevolent Irish Society, founded in 1806 to provide assistance to needy Irish residents; and the Society for Improving the Condition of the Poor in St. John's, founded by commercial and religious leaders in 1803. These initiatives were a response by the more affluent classes to the deplorable conditions which characterized St. John's during these years and to the perceived danger that those conditions presented to public order. They also underscore Newfoundland's development as a colony. As more merchants established residence in Newfoundland, the wealth generated by the fishery and trade began to grow. The number of carriages and fine houses, the number of professionals, tradesmen, artisans, and smaller businessmen, the founding of the Mercantile Society in 1806 (an organization representing the commercial point of view), the appearance of a newspaper in 1807, a public reading room before 1810, a volunteer Fire Brigade in 1811, a constabulary in 1812, even a visiting theatrical group from Québec in 1806, all confirmed that a "society" complete with a permanent resident elite was emerging in Newfoundland.

With social development also came the first expressions of dissatisfaction at government policy towards Newfoundland. Despite minor concessions, by and large the island was still governed by regulations best suited for a rapidly vanishing migratory fishery. In 1811 William Carson published the first of his "reform" tracts. While the theme of political reform belongs more properly to the next chapter, its origins before 1815 confirm how far Newfoundland had gone in its transformation from fishery to colony.

Nevertheless, that transformation was not yet complete. The desire for political and judicial reform was far from widespread, and men like William Carson did not yet belong to anything as coherent as a reform "movement." The sense of social responsibility among the "respectable classes" was still in an infant state. Governor Gambier, not the good citizens of St. John's, had been the driving force behind the establishment of Charity Schools for the poor, while the creation of a constabulary force in 1812 aroused complaints about the cost. Finally, for all its size and importance as an emporium of trade and commerce, St. John's was not yet the economic or social centre of Newfoundland. Towns like Harbour Grace and Trinity were sufficiently independent of St. John's that their local elites felt little sense of subordination to the larger town. Regular commerce between Trinity and St. John's was only just beginning. The year 1815 thus represents a convenient chronological marker, rather than a profound turning point. The residential fishery may have replaced the migratory one during the wars that closed the eighteenth century, but the transformation of the fisheries, like the transformation of Newfoundland itself, was not caused by those wars. Rather, the transformation was rooted in a whole series of complex changes that occurred throughout the eighteenth century, and which would persist into the next.

Time Line

1702	Beginning of the War of the Spanish Succession; warships under command of Captain John Leake attack French fishing stations from Trepassey to St. Pierre but avoid Plaisance.
1703	The Society for the Propagation of the Gospel, the missionary arm of the Church of England, extends its activities to Newfoundland by providing financial support to the Rev. John Jackson, the minister and garrison chaplain at St. John's.
1705	French forces from Plaisance under the command of Governor Subercase attack and destroy St. John's.
1706	British naval and military forces carry out an attack on the French fishery on the Petit Nord (Fleur de Lys to St. Anthony).
1708	An Order-in-Council places naval commodores in overall charge of the fishery. French forces from Plaisance and led by St. Ovide de Brouillan again attack and destroy St. John's.
1713	Treaty of Utrecht officially ends the War of the Spanish Succession; French must withdraw from Newfoundland but may fish on Treaty Shore from Cape Bonavista to Point Riche.
1714	French complete their withdrawal from Plaisance; British take over Placentia as well as St. Pierre and Miquelon and make Placentia the military centre of Newfoundland.
1714-1715	William Taverner conducts a survey of Placentia Bay, Burin Peninsula, and St. Pierre for the Board of Trade.
1715	Inshore fishery fails for nearly a decade; British develop offshore fishery on the banks.
1716	Lieutenant John Gaudy conducts hydrographic survey for the British Admiralty of the south coast as far as Burgeo.

1729	Naval officers stationed in Newfoundland are empowered by the government for the first time to serve as governor with full civil powers for duration of fishing season; subordinate naval officers serve as the governor's surrogates. Henry Osborne becomes first naval governor; appoints magistrates in six districts.
1739	England goes to war with Spain; an important market for fish is closed.
1741	Improvements to Fort William signal renewed attention to St. John's as military centre.
1744	France officially enters war against England; British restore role of St. John's as Newfoundland's primary military centre.
1748	Treaty of Aix-la-Chapelle ends the War of the Austrian Succession.
1750	A permanent Court of Oyer and Terminer is set up to hear cases involving capital crimes.
1751	A Vice-Admiralty Court is established in St. John's; Michael Gill is appointed Judge.
1755	Royal Navy takes pre-emptive measures against French fishery a year before war is declared.
1762	French expedition captures St. John's in June and begins destruction of inshore fishery; British counter-expedition force French to withdraw nearly three months later.
1763	Treaty of Paris brings the Seven Years' War to an end; France recovers St. Pierre and Miquelon but loses Canada and Labrador to the British. Proclamation of 1763 places Labrador under the administrative jurisdiction of the governor of Newfoundland.
1764-1767	James Cook conducts hydrographic surveys of certain coasts of Newfoundland and Labrador.
1765	With Moravian assistance, Governor Hugh Palliser negotiates a friendship treaty with Inuit on the Labrador coast.

1766	York Fort (a blockhouse) is established in Chateau Harbour for the protection of the fishery on the Labrador coast.
1768	Expedition led by Lieutenant John Cartwright into the Exploits Valley fails to make contact with the Beothuk people.
1771	Moravian mission is established at Nain.
1774	The Québec Act extends the boundaries of Québec to include Labrador.
1775	Publication of "A general chart of the Island of Newfoundland" by James Cook and Michael Lane. This is the first accurate depiction of the entire island of Newfoundland. Outbreak of American War of Independence; privateers molest fishery. Palliser's Act (Act, 15 Geo. III, c. 31) introduces, revises, and reaffirms King William's Act of 1699.
1776	Moravian mission is established at Okak.
1778	American War escalates as France declares war on Great Britain.
1782	Moravian mission is established at Hopedale.
1783	Treaty of Versaillés ends war between France and England; Treaty Shore is redefined, now extending from Cape St. John to Cape Ray.
1784	Governor Campbell formally proclaims freedom of religion and of conscience in Newfoundland. Reverend James O'Donel, holding the rank of Prefect-Apostolic, arrives in St. John's as the first officially sanctioned Roman Catholic priest in Newfoundland.
1787	Richard Hutchings successfully challenges the judicial practice of naval surrogates.
1789	French Revolution begins; revolution and war will bring a virtual end to the French fishery for over twenty-five years.
1791	Establishment of a Court of Civil Jurisdiction for one year.

1792	Establishment of an annually renewable "Supreme Court of Judicature of the Island of Newfoundland" and a system of surrogate courts; John Reeves appointed first Chief Justice.
1793	Birth of commercial seal fishery when schooners push into pack ice in pursuit of seals for first time; a Parliamentary Commission is established to enquire into the decline of the migratory fishery; outbreak of French Revolutionary wars.
1796	Reverend James O'Donel becomes Newfoundland's first Catholic bishop; French Admiral de Richery attacks the fishery; St. John's defences cannot prevent destruction of Petty Harbour, Bay Bulls, other nearby fishing centres.
1797	The Great (Naval) Mutiny in England comes to Newfoundland when sailors on HMS *Latona* in St. John's harbour threaten mutiny; it is quickly suppressed.
1800	Plot by Irish soldiers of the Newfoundland Regiment to mutiny is exposed by Bishop O'Donel.
1809	Judicial system of Newfoundland is made permanent; British government restores Labrador to the authority of Newfoundland.
1811	Captain David Buchan leads expedition into the interior in an attempt to contact the Beothuk people.
1812	War breaks out between Great Britain and the United States.
1815	End of the Napoleonic Wars.

CHAPTER IV

The Nineteenth Century, 1815-1914

James K. Hiller

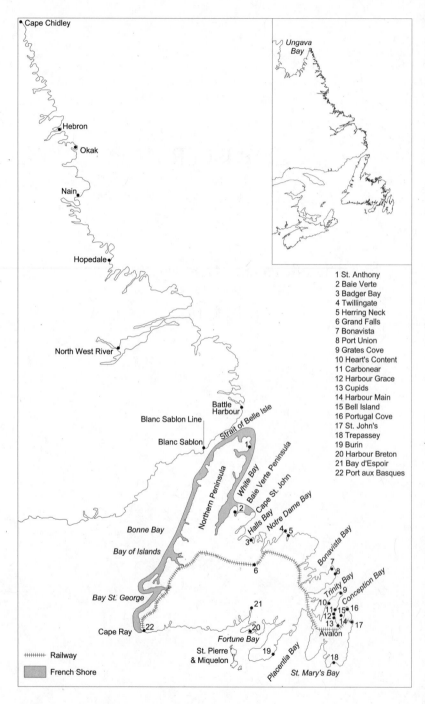

Settlement areas and the railway in the late nineteenth century.

Newfoundland emerged as a country during the century between the end of the Anglo-French wars in 1815 and the outbreak of the Great War in 1914. At the start of the period it was still viewed from Britain as a fishing station under naval administration. Yet Newfoundland was entering a new phase in its history with the establishment of a colonial society and economy, and its place in the Atlantic world was changing. By 1914, Newfoundland was a dominion in all but name: its prime ministers attended imperial conferences; its economy was more diversified; and its people had developed a distinct culture and identity. It was also much more closely linked to the mainland, especially to what had become the Dominion of Canada in 1867. Newfoundland had become more North American than North Atlantic in its orientation.

These trends, as the previous chapter has shown, started in the later eighteenth century and intensified during the twenty-plus years of war between Britain and France. A resident fishery replaced the English migratory fishery, which supported a substantial, if scattered, permanent population of approximately 40,000. Firms based in Britain still dominated the trade in 1815, and transatlantic links remained strong and active, but from the British government's perspective Newfoundland was no longer the important component of the Empire that it once had been. Victory over France had established Britain as the dominant western power with unchallenged economic and naval supremacy. In this new scheme of things, Newfoundland was no longer needed as a nursery for seamen, insofar as it ever had been, and its fisheries were of relatively minor economic significance. As well, because of its limited agricultural potential and small population, Newfoundland did not seriously compete either as a destination for British emigrants or as a market for British exports. Once an imperial prize, Newfoundland was in danger of becoming an imperial backwater.

The residents in 1815 were mainly recent immigrants of English and Irish origin who had yet to develop a distinctive identity as Newfoundlanders. Most of the island's coastline, outside the area between Cape St. John and Bay d'Espoir, was sparsely populated, and the interior was the preserve of the Mi'kmaq and of a remnant of the Beothuk people. St. John's was the administrative, military, and political centre, but it was not yet economically and financially dominant.

The Baie Verte and Northern Peninsulas, White Bay, and the west coast as far south as Cape Ray comprised the French Shore. Here, under eighteenth-century Anglo-French treaties renewed in 1815, the French could fish in season. The extent of that right or privilege was fiercely disputed during the nineteenth century, and many Newfoundlanders also came to resent the return to France of the islands of St. Pierre and Miquelon. Another potential irritant lay in the 1818 fisheries convention between Britain and the United States, which allowed Americans to fish on the island's coasts facing the Gulf of St. Lawrence, and at Labrador.

Gravestone of Elias Piccot, Portugal Cove, "who died the 2nd of March 1818 / Aged 63 years" (photo: Norah Renouf, Newfoundland Historical Society).

The "Coast of Labrador" had been returned to Newfoundland jurisdiction in 1809. The coastal limits were set in 1825 from Blanc Sablon to "the entrance to Hudson's Straits," which (for reasons that are unclear) was eventually located at Cape Chidley. The interior boundary was undefined. In the north, Moravian mission stations at Hopedale, Nain, and Okak ministered to the nearby Inuit. Innu bands hunted and fished in the interior, and a Métis population of mixed descent was becoming established in the central region. In the south and along the Strait of Belle Isle, fishing and trading establishments run by Jersey and Newfoundland firms supported a small European population of fishers, trappers, and hunters. A Newfoundland-based migratory fishery developed at Labrador after 1815, when Newfoundlanders fishing on the French Shore were forced to leave by the returning French fishing fleet.

The apparatus of the eighteenth-century "naval state" remained in place. There were courts, magistrates, a few clergymen (both Roman Catholic and Protestant), and a small cadre of permanent officials. There was a customs house, and fortifications and a military garrison in St. John's. The governor was the commodore of the Royal Navy squadron, and he did not remain for the winter. There was no legislature, not even a formal council to advise the governors who assumed they could rule by issuing proclamations. It was a system that had become anachronistic, as was clearly demonstrated with the crisis that engulfed Newfoundland when the wars ended in 1815.

Crisis and Reform

With the return of peace the price of fish collapsed, causing bankruptcies, poverty, and destitution. There was unrest and violence, aggravated by food shortages, severe winters, and by fires in St. John's. Yet immigrants continued

Preparation of fish, Cap-Rouge, 1857-1859 (photo: Paul-Émile Miot, courtesy of Library and Archives Canada).

to arrive, mainly from southeast Ireland, which made the situation even worse. The British government reacted slowly, and initially ordered the governor to stay year-round to deal with the crisis—the first, Sir Francis Pickmore, died in the attempt during the hard winter of 1817-1818. But for the middle class of St. John's, this was not enough. With the Scottish-born Dr. William Carson and later the Irish merchant Patrick Morris as their spokesmen, activists lobbied for the end of the naval state. Newfoundland, they argued, should be treated in the same way as the other British North American colonies, and its residents should enjoy the same rights as British subjects elsewhere in the Empire. Eventually, in 1824, the old fisheries laws were repealed and Newfoundland became a Crown Colony. Sir Thomas Cochrane, the first civil governor, took office in 1825, and the present Government House began to rise on the barrens behind the ramshackle town.

The British government hesitated to give Newfoundland a legislature, thinking that the educated element in the population was too small, and the society in general too new and too divided between English and Irish and Protestant and Roman Catholic. Some outport firms opposed these proposed political changes, seeing them as a St. John's power grab. However, the campaign for representative government was supported by a broad spectrum of professionals and merchants and, in the process, an attractive but inaccurate interpretation of Newfoundland and its history became articulated and embedded, which was to survive into the twenty-first century.

In this romanticized version of events, Newfoundland was ever the victim of the imperial government and the West Country merchants, interests that valued the fisheries but nothing else about the country. To promote the migratory fishery, settlement was forbidden, residents were harassed by

View from the north side of Government House, pre-1901 (Archives and Manuscripts, Memorial University Library).

fishing admirals and the Navy, their houses were torn down, and agriculture and other economic activities were proscribed. Early government had been authoritarian, minimal, and erratic. In spite of it all, the hardy settlers—the planters—had stood their ground and survived to found a new society in a country which was undeveloped, with a small population and untouched landward resources. This state of affairs was the result of British indifference and neglect, and the solution lay in local control. Once that was achieved, the country would become "rich and great," as Carson put it. He and his colleagues spoke, of course, without knowing what landward resources Newfoundland and Labrador actually possessed, since no surveys had been carried out. Nevertheless, they confidently predicted the existence of hitherto undiscovered resources, agricultural and mineral—an assumption which was to have a long life.

A legislature met for the first time in 1832. It consisted of a fifteen-member House of Assembly, elected by male householders, representing nine districts. Labrador, the French Shore, and the southwest coast were not included. The Legislative Council formed the appointed upper house, most of whose members also served on the Executive Council which was the colony's executive government and was chaired by the governor. This was the beginning of formal Newfoundland politics. There was no legislative building until the Colonial Building opened in 1850, and the first Assembly met in a St. John's tavern owned by a Mrs. Mary Travers.

The new constitution soon exposed the fissures in a Newfoundland society still in the process of formation. Most obvious was the ethnic and sectarian split between residents of English and Irish birth or descent. The Roman Catholic bishop, Michael Anthony Fleming, thought that priests had a duty to act politically when necessary, and actively intervened in elections to ensure that his candidates were successful. This in turn prompted a vigorous Protestant reaction, hardly surprising given the prevalence of anti-Catholic and anti-Irish sentiment in this period. Sectarianism thus entered Newfoundland

---

Lundrigan and Butler

In May 1819, a merchant brought an action for debt against James Lundrigan, a fisherman living in Cupids. The case was heard by a surrogate magistrate, in this case a Church of England clergyman. He decided in the merchant's favour, and Lundrigan's house, fishing room, and boat were attached and sold to one of the merchant's clerks. When the constable went to Cupids to take possession of the house, however, Lundrigan's wife threatened to "blow his brains out." The constable retreated. The following year, another surrogate court summoned Lundrigan to appear. He refused, was arrested, and held on board HMS *Grasshopper*. On 6 July, the surrogates sentenced Lundrigan to thirty-six lashes on his bare back for contempt, and ordered the immediate possession of his premises. He fainted after fourteen lashes, and the family was evicted. The next day, in Harbour Main, Philip Butler was also sentenced to thirty-six lashes for contempt, and received twelve. His wife, like Lundrigan's, refused to vacate the house; whereupon the door was broken down and the family ejected.

The St. John's reformers made the harsh treatment of the two lowly fishermen into a *cause célèbre*, symbolizing the need for change. Supported by the reformers, Lundrigan and Butler sued the surrogates and claimed damages. They lost, but the juries and the Chief Justice strongly condemned the surrogates' actions, and the reformers had gained the momentum they needed. The agitation was now underway that would lead to the reforms of 1824 and 1832.

---

politics at the start, and elections became rowdy affairs, especially in St. John's and Conception Bay, as reformers and radicals—known generally as liberals—fought conservative supporters of the colonial establishment. The former were mainly Roman Catholics, and the conservatives mainly Protestants, backed by the larger mercantile houses in St. John's and the major outports. The Protestant clergy tended to be more discreet than their Catholic counterparts, but were certainly involved.

There were other tensions as well. Within the Protestant fold, an increasing number of Methodists drew apart from the Church of England once Bishop Edward Feild began to introduce high church doctrine and practice in the 1840s. High churchmen like Feild saw their church as Catholic, though not Roman, and were not interested in fraternal cooperation with the Methodists and other dissenting Protestants. A tension also existed between native-born Newfoundlanders (whatever their origins) and newer arrivals. "Newfoundlanders" tended to resent the success and condescension of immigrants, and formed a non-denominational Natives' Society in the early 1840s, whose colours were red, white, and green. Roman Catholic natives also tended to resist clerical control. In addition, there were the stresses of economic disparity and social class between fishermen and merchants.

Economic Issues

This brings us to the economy of nineteenth-century Newfoundland. The seasonal round on the east coast began with the seal fishery. Seal oil was a valued commodity used for lighting and lubrication, and seal pelts

Sealing Disasters, 1914

A storm in late March 1914 was one cause of the heavy loss of life at the seal fishery that year. The loss of the SS *Southern Cross* was the largest single disaster in the industry's history. Under the command of Captain George Clarke of Brigus, the steamer sailed to the Gulf with a crew of 173 men, most of them young, and from Conception Bay. Returning with a full load of pelts, the *Southern Cross* ran into the storm as it neared Cape Pine. It was seen by another steamer at 1100 on 31 March, but then disappeared. There were no survivors.

The other famous disaster that year involved the crew of the SS *Newfoundland*, commanded by Captain Westbury Kean. The *Newfoundland* became jammed in the ice, several miles away from other vessels. On 30 March, Wes Kean's father, Captain Abram Kean of the *Stephano*, signalled that he had found seals. Wes Kean told his crew to walk to the *Stephano*, and they set off early the next morning. Abram Kean took them to a patch of seals, and told them to return to the *Newfoundland* when

they had finished—even though the weather was getting worse, and they were a long way from their ship. As they walked back, they were engulfed by the storm. They spent fifty-three hours on the ice, while each captain thought the men were on the other's ship. Seventy-eight men died from exposure or drowning, and eleven were permanently disabled. The bodies, "stacked like cordwood," were taken back to St. John's by the SS *Bellaventure*.

Sealers on ice (photo: S.R. Oakley, courtesy of Archives and Manuscripts, Memorial University Library).

were manufactured into low-grade leather. In northern Newfoundland and southern Labrador, migrating harp seals were taken in nets. Seals whelping on the ice floes in the spring were sometimes taken by landsmen in boats but were mainly caught by schooners which sailed to the ice to find the "main patch." Sealing was a bloody affair, but it could be lucrative, and the fishery established the sealer as an heroic figure in Newfoundland folklore. Sealing was centrally important to the Newfoundland economy in the first half of the nineteenth century, employing some 370 vessels and 14,000 men in the late 1850s; the annual take was some 400,000 seals valued at $1.4 million. By this time the seal herds were under pressure, and outfitters then turned to larger vessels which could manoeuvre in the ice more efficiently than schooners—first brigs and brigantines and then, in the 1860s, steamers. As a result the seal fishery became centralized in St. John's and Harbour Grace, and employed significantly fewer men—3,600 by the late 1890s, bringing in 270,000 seals valued at $477,500. From the 1870s a drop in demand for seal oil caused the industry to contract significantly, and this was a serious blow to the east coast economy.

Survivors of the 1914 *Newfoundland* disaster being taken ashore from the *Bellaventure* in St. John's harbour (Archives and Manuscripts, Memorial University Library).

On the south coast, the main spring industry was the catching of herring and capelin for sale to banking vessels from France, Nova Scotia, and New England, for use as bait on the long lines of hooks used in the offshore fishery. This was a valuable trade, and much of it took place at St. Pierre, where south coast Newfoundlanders also sold wood, meat, and other items. The St. Pierre trade bothered the authorities and merchants in St. John's, since smuggling was widespread and profits went elsewhere.

Newfoundlanders did not participate significantly in the bank fishery until the 1880s, and until then the cod fishery was carried on inshore. Fishers used jiggers, seines, long lines, and, from the 1860s, cod traps. The Labrador fishery grew in importance during the century, and extended further and further north. Some schooners known as floaters followed the fish and took their catch back to Newfoundland ports. Other crews, the stationers, fished from fixed locations and were often transported to Labrador by others. It was a local facsimile of the old migratory fishery.

Fishing crews were family-based, in contrast to the master-servant relationship which had existed in the eighteenth century, with women playing an important role in curing the fish after it had been caught, split, and salted by the men. Women also looked after the household and the gardens. It was a life characterized by hard and constant work which depended on a credit relationship with a merchant, since outport fishing families were not self-sufficient. Although a family could grow vegetables, pick berries, keep some livestock, cut firewood, make their own clothes, and build their own houses and vessels, they could not produce items such as cloth, tea, molasses, ropes and twines, nails, glass, sailcloth, cod traps, and, later, gasoline engines. The fish they caught (and any other marketable goods) enabled them to buy what

William Grey, "Battle Harbour, Labrador," from *Sketches of Newfoundland and Labrador* (Anastatic Press, 1858) (Centre for Newfoundland Studies).

they could not produce on a credit basis, and cash was not involved. The merchant advanced supplies against the proceeds of a crew's voyage, and settled up at the end of the season.

That this was an unequal relationship is obvious, but how far it was always oppressive and exploitative is less clear. Merchants unilaterally set prices for supplies and for fish, could cull (sort) fish as they saw fit, and could terminate or restrict credit if they chose. On the other hand, they needed to keep productive fishermen on their books, and were well aware that fishermen could—depending on where they lived—deal with more than one buyer, and earn income through sales to foreign vessels and passing traders, or by working on roads and, later, railways. There were always opportunities on the mainland as well.

Having bought the fish from his dealers, it was the merchant's job to send it to market. The best fish went to Spain and Portugal, lower grades to other Mediterranean markets and the West Indies. Salt fish was not a high-priced commodity, and profits could be thin or non-existent. Prices fluctuated according to the catch, competition, and demand, and the merchants themselves depended on credit from local banks, which bridged them over the months that elapsed between the purchase of a cargo of fish and its eventual sale. It was a risky business and, contrary to common assumptions, few if any fish merchants made fortunes in this period: indeed, they were lucky to survive. Much more research is needed, but it is clear nevertheless that the stark picture of poverty-stricken fishing families being exploited and oppressed by rich merchants requires modification.

The urban economy of St. John's was, of course, somewhat different. The departure of the British military garrison in 1870 was a blow, but by this time "Water Street" (a phrase which, like "Bay Street," "Wall Street," or "the

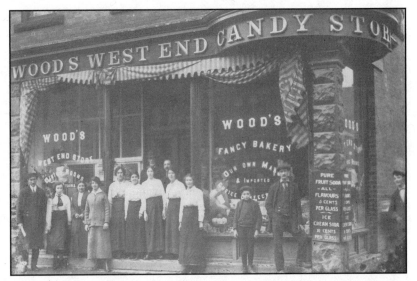

Wood's West End Candy Store and Dining Rooms, c. 1900, was located on Water Street in St. John's (Provincial Archives of Newfoundland and Labrador).

City," captures a certain economic interest group) had taken over most of the Newfoundland economy. The independent, outport-based West Country and Jersey firms had disappeared, with the exception of Newman and Company, which still carried on business at Harbour Breton and St. John's. The major St. John's mercantile houses operated branches and subsidiaries around the island and in southern Labrador, and Water Street controlled the Union and Commercial banks and the Chamber of Commerce. St. John's was now the colony's entrepôt, where fish and seal products were traded and exported, where imported goods arrived, where major financial and legal transactions took place, and where businessmen interacted with the colonial government and its bureaucracy. St. John's was the seat of government, the headquarters of the churches and their colleges were located there, as were the major newspapers. Though Harbour Grace, Carbonear, Burin, Twillingate, and other regional centres remained important mercantile and administrative hubs for some time, St. John's had become the undisputed and sometimes resented capital. The colony's middle and upper classes clustered on the upper levels of the steep hill on the north side of the harbour, and it was they who were to define the country's future.

Responsible Government

During the mid-nineteenth century, these elites managed the evolution of agreements and understandings that made this new colonial society work. The issue of responsible government, which meant an Executive Council responsible to the House of Assembly rather than directly to the Crown, had a great deal to do with this. The drive for this change, which was also occurring in most British colonies of settlement, was spearheaded by Liberals seeking home rule for the Newfoundland Irish, but they were supported by the Methodist community, as both groups resented exclusion from place and patronage. It proved to be a tense and strenuous fight, but these uneasy allies eventually convinced a reluctant Colonial Office that political change had to come. Responsible government appeared in 1855, and the triumphant Liberals took office. The first premier was Philip Little, a Prince Edward Islander and the first Catholic lawyer to practise in Newfoundland.

As the dust settled, the basis of the Newfoundland state that was to last until 1934 began to emerge. It had a number of unusual features, some of which derived from an understanding that Newfoundland best functioned through interlocking relationships between the elected government, the mercantile interest, and the major churches. Water Street spoke through the Chamber of Commerce (later the Board of Trade). Then, as now, businessmen did not want government interference in 'their' preserve. The job of the government was to do what the fish trade wanted, not to busy itself with intrusive regulation. By and large the pervasiveness of laissez-faire ideology and the influence of Water Street meant that governments generally accepted the principle of non-interference until the 1920s, though a lack of money and effective government machinery also blunted the ability to intervene, even had they wanted to.

As for the churches, they were allowed to control the education system. In an age when religion and education were intertwined, Newfoundland's pragmatic answer to the question of how to provide education to the maximum number of children with the least amount of controversy was to divide the education grant between the three major denominations (more were added later), and establish a denominational education system under loose government supervision. The process began in 1843, when separate Catholic and Protestant systems were created, and ended thirty years later when the legislature split the Protestant education grant between the Methodists and the Church of England. There was no Ministry of Education until 1920. In addition, the churches policed the unwritten agreement which emerged in the 1860s that each denomination should be proportionately represented in the Executive Council, the legislature, the courts, and the civil service. If one-third of the population was Methodist, for example, then this fact should be reflected in place, pay, and patronage. As a result, census-taking became a fraught business since each denomination wanted to maximize its count, and the deal did not eliminate sectarian rivalries and prejudices which persisted for many years. Overall, though, this was a sensible move to try and remove sectarian feuding from politics, and it largely succeeded. Specifically Catholic and Protestant political parties eventually disappeared, and the elites observed the rules of the game.

Population by Census Years (from the Census of Newfoundland, 1857-1911)

	1857	1869	1874	1884	1891	1901	1911
Total	124,288	146,536	161,968	197,355	202,040	220,984	242,619
% Roman Catholic	45.8	41.7	39.7	38.1	36	34.4	33.5
% Protestant	54.2	58.3	60.3	61.9	64	65.6	66.5

Two other features of responsible government in Newfoundland deserve comment. The small and scattered population meant that there were no elected local governments and no local taxation, except in St. John's where a municipal board was established in 1888. The central government collected all the revenue, mainly from duties, and doled it out, administering local affairs through the magistrates and appointed road and school boards. The result was a highly centralized system in which there were numerous opportunities for political manipulation. Members of the House of Assembly became the ambassadors and advocates for their districts in St. John's—the essential links between centre and periphery. The system may have been practical, but it reinforced the dominance of St. John's while allowing political patronage to become rampant.

Second, the authority of the colonial government was significantly restricted by the pre-existing British fisheries treaties with France and the United States, mentioned above. The French Shore issue in particular became a focus for nascent Newfoundland nationalism, and a major political issue. France claimed that its fishery on the French Shore was exclusive, that only French subjects could legally fish there in season, and that British subjects could neither settle nor fish there without French permission. The Newfoundland government had no business there, either. Newfoundlanders argued that the fishery was concurrent, and that British subjects could do whatever they wanted on the French Shore so long as the French fishery was uninterrupted. The British government prevaricated, vacillated, and eventually concluded a deal with France in 1857 which, it thought, would satisfy all parties.

Nationalism, Confederation, and Railways

The 1857 French Shore convention was the first major problem that the newly minted Liberal administration elected in 1855 had to face. The terms of the draft convention, which seemed eminently practical and reasonable in Europe, proved to be unacceptable in Newfoundland. Outraged spokesmen of all parties and creeds agreed that too much had been conceded for too little, and the colony refused assent. That the British government then withdrew the convention and promised that the colony's "maritime or territorial rights" would not in future be modified without its consent was seen as a famous national victory, and was long remembered.

Nascent nationalism was also stimulated by the debate some years later over whether Newfoundland should be a founding member of the Canadian confederation. The colony was not invited to send representatives to the Charlottetown conference in 1864, and in effect invited itself to the subsequent Québec conference where it was included in the famous founding resolutions. However, it is clear that the Canada originally envisioned by the fathers of confederation did not include Newfoundland, except as an afterthought. Small wonder, then, that the idea of confederation was received in the colony with considerable ambivalence. Nevertheless, the 1860s was an economically miserable decade, pessimism about the future was widespread, and confederation seemed to some to be an attractive option. But this proved to be a minority view. An unlikely coalition of Roman Catholic Liberals and Conservative merchants, old enemies, created an anti-confederate party, led by the elderly but energetic merchant, Charles Fox Bennett. The Liberals thought that within confederation they might lose what they had achieved—separate Catholic schools, for instance, and access to place and power. Moreover, confederation recalled the hated Anglo-Irish union on which Ireland's ills were usually blamed. Merchants, whose influence in the age of open voting was considerable, feared increased taxation and protective tariffs which would dislocate traditional trade patterns. All in all, the anti-confederates argued (with some justification) that confederation was a central Canadian concoction which had little to offer Newfoundland other than increased taxation. The confederates found it difficult to counter these arguments, and were soundly defeated in the 1869 general election which was, in effect, a confederation referendum. Most Newfoundlanders obviously believed that their country had the resources with which to underpin political independence within the British Empire, but poverty was widespread, emigration was growing, and the fisheries alone seemed unable to support a growing population. So what was the way forward? One answer was that the government should take the lead in stimulating economic diversification. The reports of the Geological Survey, headed by Alexander Murray and begun in 1864, were highly optimistic and predicted mines, forest industries, and agricultural settlements—land-based developments which would end total reliance on the fisheries. The west coast was thought to be a particularly promising area for future growth. Access to these resources could be provided by a railway, steam being the contemporary symbol of progress and modernity. By the late 1870s a political realignment had brought together the Liberals and a wing of the Conservatives behind a progressive agenda which looked to a trans-island railway as the key to the future. In time, this coalition adopted the name "Liberal." Those who were skeptical about this programme eventually became known as the Tory party, which fought to focus attention on the fisheries and on the threat posed by French competition in European markets. Tories were less populist and feared that the cost of railway building would drive the colony into confederation.

Interior view of fishing stage, French Shore, Newfoundland, 1857 (photo: Paul-Émile Miot, courtesy of Library and Archives Canada).

These issues defined colonial politics for the rest of the century, accentuated and distorted by local quarrels and a deteriorating economic situation.

The railway was built in two phases. In 1881, after intense and divisive debate, Sir William Whiteway's government awarded a contract to the New York-based Newfoundland Railway Company. It was to build a narrow-gauge railway from St. John's to Hall's Bay, then the centre of an active copper-mining region. The original idea of a trans-island line was shelved because the British government would not allow railway building or a terminus on the French Shore. The company was to raise the capital and own the track. Construction began that year, the line running from a terminus at Fort William and along what is now Empire Avenue before crossing to Conception Bay. By 1885 trains were running between St. John's and Harbour Grace, but the company was bankrupt.

The second phase began with Whiteway's victory in the 1889 election, and the signature the next year of a contract with Robert G. Reid. Originally from Scotland, Reid was an experienced railway contractor based in Montreal. He agreed to complete the Hall's Bay railway at a cost of $15,600 per mile. In 1893 he agreed to continue the line on the same terms to the west coast—the British having given permission—and would operate the railway for ten years in return for land grants of 5,000 acres per mile.

Problems in the Fishery

Reid proved to be reliable and efficient, but the cost of railway building steadily drove up the public debt and helped create an atmosphere of financial instability. Yet the railway was not the only factor. The last quarter of the nineteenth century saw falling prices for all primary products, which obviously hurt Newfoundland. The seal fishery was in decline, and, as for salt

Cod drying on flakes at Quidi Vidi Lake, c. 1886 (photo: Simeon Parsons, courtesy of Library and Archives Canada).

fish, exporters faced falling prices in Europe where French and Norwegian fish was entering traditional Newfoundland markets in large volumes. Not surprisingly, there was extensive discussion about what was going wrong. Some blamed the competition, focusing their indignation on France, which heavily subsidized its fisheries. French fishermen took cod not only on the hated French Shore, but increasingly on the Grand Banks, using St. Pierre as a base, and using Newfoundland bait. The catch would then appear in Spain or Italy, and undersell the Newfoundland product. Norway, in contrast, was viewed as a "fair" competitor.

Another issue was quality. The Newfoundland fishery was based on hundreds of family-centred crews. Each crew caught the fish, processed and cured it, and sold it to a merchant. This structure meant that there was no way to standardize the product. Each crew produced its own cure, and each merchant graded the fish as he chose. The uncertainty of the cull reduced the incentive to produce high quality fish (if Number One fish might be graded as the inferior West India, what was the point in trying to produce a higher quality?), and the problem was intensified by the introduction of "tal qual" buying. This meant fish was purchased at a flat price regardless of quality. Such developments encouraged the assumption that salt fish was not so much an article of food as a medium of exchange, which further militated against a consistently high quality product.

Since foreign buyers could not be confident that they would receive what they had ordered and expected, they began to insist on consignment sales, that is, they would await a cargo's arrival before agreeing to a price. Disorganized marketing only made matters worse. Exporters wanted to get fish to market as soon as possible, in order to get the best price. So the temptation was to buy fish tal qual or before it was ready, and rush it off. The best strategy for a buyer, obviously, was to wait until several competing Newfoundland freighters were in port (let alone French and Norwegian shipments) and

Five men camping at Nine Mile Post, Placentia Railway Line, 1904 (Archives and Manuscripts, Memorial University Library).

see what happened. The colony's market share in Europe began to slip, and mercantile bank debt climbed at the same time as the government itself was becoming reliant on annual loan flotations.

The Politics of Bait

The economic situation focused attention on the colony's stocks of bait fishes—herring, capelin, and squid—which were, as we have seen, relied on by foreign and Canadian vessels fishing on the banks. If the colony could control the sale and export of bait, it was argued, then it would possess a valuable weapon and bargaining chip. Thus a Bait Act was passed in 1887, to which the British government reluctantly assented. The aim of its promoters was primarily to cripple the French bank fishery, and weaken St. Pierre's position as a trading and fishing centre. However, bait might also be used to gain access to the United States market. American vessels could have access to Newfoundland bait, and, in return, the United States would give free entry to Newfoundland products.

The French government saw the Bait Act as a declaration of war. Even though the Act failed to harm the French bank fishery in any significant way, it did hurt the economy of St. Pierre and Miquelon. The French Shore became of greater importance to France than it had been for some time as a place where banking vessels could find bait if need be and where St. Pierrais could both fish cod and take lobster.

At this time the west coast lobster fishery was becoming important, and the French wanted a share. Newfoundlanders opposed this, arguing that the French could not legally take lobsters since they were not fish. The French replied that lobsters were fish within the meaning of the treaties which allowed them to take anything that was in the sea. Moreover, if Newfoundlanders could can lobsters, so could the French. This arcane dispute rumbled on for some time, and as a temporary solution the British and French governments agreed to a *modus vivendi* (1890) whereby the lobster fishery would be supervised by the two naval squadrons which patrolled the French Shore each year. The Newfoundland government was outraged (with reason), and there was much jubilation when the British commodore was charged with trespass for closing down a Newfoundland-owned lobster cannery (locally known as a "factory") in St. George's Bay. This turn of events rattled the British government, which discovered that it had no statutory authority to enforce the *modus* or any other treaty regulations on the French Shore. A standoff between the colonial and imperial governments ended when the colony eventually agreed to pass the necessary enforcement legislation—otherwise the British Parliament would have done so—but only on an annual basis.

The tensions generated by this dispute were heightened by an uproar over reciprocity with the United States. In 1890, the rising political star Robert Bond went to Washington (with British permission) and successfully negotiated a draft trade agreement which came to be known as the Bond-Blaine treaty. The external relations of all British colonies were controlled by the British government, and when the Canadian government woke up to what was happening, it vigorously protested to the Colonial Office. Previous trade and fisheries agreements with the United States had been made with British North America as a whole. For Newfoundland to arrange a separate agreement was to breach the common front and hurt Canada's chance of a similar deal. It might also fuel the repeal movement in Nova Scotia which would be able to argue that Newfoundland did better by staying out of confederation than did Nova Scotia by staying in. London listened and the treaty was dead. Canada and Newfoundland might have had equal status within the Empire, but certainly not the same importance. Furious, Bond persuaded the government to retaliate against Canada and a brief tariff war resulted. Canada refused to alter its position, hinting that the best solution might be confederation. In these circumstances, this was not on the cards.

The Crisis of the 1890s

The colony's leaders were distracted from further international confrontations (which made the colony unpopular with the British government) by the great fire which destroyed much of St. John's on 8 July 1892, and then by perhaps the most saucy political manoeuvre in the country's political history. Defeated in the 1893 general election, the Tories alleged that many government members had won their seats by indulging in corrupt practices, and petitioned the Supreme Court accordingly. To everyone's surprise the court agreed, and during the spring and summer of 1894 a parade of Liberal MHAs, including Whiteway and Bond, found themselves unseated and disqualified, essentially for running their election campaigns in the usual way. The Tories temporarily took over the government, but they had to schedule by-elections for the vacant seats. They lost most of these, so that by early 1895 the Liberals were back, just in time to deal with the fallout from the closure of the Union and the Commercial banks on 10 December 1894.

The banks had loaned too much money to a fish trade that was in trouble, and were unable to collect most of their debts—merchants had plenty of fish, but few liquid assets. Shareholders and depositors stood to lose a great deal of money, the banks'

Duckworth Street and city ruins looking west after the fire of 1892 (Archives and Manuscripts, Memorial University Library).

mercantile creditors faced ruin, and the government found itself on the edge of bankruptcy. The impact of the so-called bank crash has never been adequately studied, but two points can be made. First, the prompt arrival of Canadian banks in St. John's meant that Newfoundland's currency became tied to the Canadian dollar, and that Canadian fiscal policy would prevail here. The government itself now dealt with the Bank of Montreal, with which R.G. Reid was closely associated. Second, there was a thorough shakeout within the fishing industry. Many firms had to sell off some or all of their assets, and some disappeared altogether, such as Munns in Harbour Grace, and Duders in Notre Dame Bay. The result seems to have been that St. John's houses retreated from direct business in the outports, becoming exporters and retailers, leaving it to smaller local merchants to supply fishermen.

The beleaguered government, still led by Whiteway, decided to send a delegation to Ottawa to investigate confederation. The talks failed. The Canadian government was cautious and stingy, the British government refused to provide a financial dowry, and most Newfoundlanders were unenthusiastic. Bond (with Reid's help) eventually saved the day by negotiating loans which shored up both the government and its Savings Bank, a coup which gained him great political kudos.

There was more excitement to come. The year 1897 saw the enthusiastic celebration of Queen Victoria's jubilee, ceremonies to mark the 400th anniversary of John Cabot's arrival, which included laying the foundation stone of Cabot Tower in St. John's, the completion of the railway to Port aux Basques, and a general election which legitimately brought the Tories to power again. One of the new government's most immediate problems

Cabot Tower and Signal Hill

The name "Signal Hill" was in use by the 1760s, recognizing the existence on the summit of a signal station operated by the military garrison since the early years of the eighteenth century. In the nineteenth century, signalling was taken over by the mercantile community in St. John's. Each firm had its own flag, which the signalman hoisted as one of its vessels approached. Vessels would also signal if they were coming from a foreign port, or needed a pilot.

Cabot Tower was built as a permanent signal station (its predecessors had been wooden blockhouses) to commemorate the 60th year of Queen Victoria's reign, and the 400th anniversary of John Cabot's voyage. Bishop Michael Howley produced the original castellated concept, which was ambitious in size and scope. The St. John's architect W.H.

Cabot Tower, shortly after its opening in 1897.

Greene modified the design to fit the budget and site, and the foundation stone was laid on 22 June 1897. It opened in 1900, and flag signalling continued there until 1958 and the creation of the Signal Hill National Historic Park.

The signalman also fired a noonday gun, which annoyed some clergymen because it interrupted their sermons. The Sunday gun ended, leading M.A. Devine to write one of his most amusing verses, "Who Stopped the Gun?"

---

was the future of the railway, which ran across the island through nowhere, and seemed destined to be a money-losing proposition. The Tories therefore decided to sell the railway to Reid for $1 million, together with the St. John's dry dock and the government telegraph system. The package included additional land grants and other franchises.

The deal is worth examining, since it posed a basic question which is still with us: what price should the country have to pay for economic development? The contract's supporters (which included a Liberal faction led by the senior St. John's MHA Edward Morris) claimed that it transferred the risks of railway operation to the Reid family, which now had a vested interest in promoting developments which would generate traffic. The colony was off the hook, apart from servicing the considerable debt incurred by the railway's construction, and the Reids would be the catalyst for economic diversification. Opponents, headed by Bond (now Liberal leader), argued that the deal was an immoral sellout, and an abdication of responsibility. The future of the country was being assigned to a private interest which might become more powerful than the elected government. Was Newfoundland to become a company colony like Rhodesia, while paying for the privilege? Surely Newfoundlanders should control their own future. There was merit in each argument, but Bond's patriotic campaign prevailed. The Tories disintegrated,

"The Newfoundland election trials: Mr. Justice Little delivering judgment." A copy of a drawing from an unknown newspaper, c. 1894 (Archives and Manuscripts, Memorial University Library).

and early in 1900 Bond won a non-confidence motion. Premier Bond, as he now was, set out to modify the Reid deal, and this was done in 1901.

As the government changed, the recession of the late nineteenth century lifted. Prices for fish and other Newfoundland products improved, and optimism began to prevail. Indeed, the period between 1900 and the Great War has been seen in retrospect as a "golden age." Iron mines opened and expanded on Bell Island. Stimulated by the railway, forest industries developed. First, sawmilling establishments opened along the line and then, in 1905, the government concluded an agreement with the Harmsworth newspaper empire in England for a pulp and paper mill at Grand Falls which, like the 1898 railway contract, was criticized for giving too much away for too little in return. The French Shore dispute was finally settled in 1904 as part of a package deal between Britain and France known as the *entente cordiale*. France gave up its treaty rights in exchange for financial compensation for the fishermen affected, and territory in west Africa. As a result the much-touted resources of western Newfoundland were now opened for development. There was a genuine sense that a past characterized by struggle, adversity, and hardship had been overcome, and that the future looked bright. Small wonder then that Governor Cavendish Boyle's "Ode to Newfoundland" received such an enthusiastic reception in 1902, as did Bishop Howley's hymn to "The Flag of Newfoundland," which he claimed to be the Pink, White, and Green. The newly founded *Newfoundland Quarterly* was filled with patriotic verses, and the Newfoundland Historical Society began its long and distinguished career. A museum was built on Duckworth Street, the frieze on its facade representing mining, forestry, and the fishery, with Britannia presiding over all.

St. John's dry dock under construction, c. 1880s (Archives and Manuscripts, Memorial University Library).

There were skeptics, among them Wilfred Grenfell, the English medical missionary who first visited Newfoundland and Labrador in 1892. Another was William Coaker, who founded the Fishermen's Protective Union (FPU) at Herring Neck in 1908. Each of them, from different perspectives, complained about the exploitation of working people in the outports. They both agreed that there were serious problems implicit in the credit system; that denominational education did not serve the outports well; and that the colonial government did not provide adequate services in rural Newfoundland and Labrador. Their solutions were different.

Grenfell charged ahead, founding a mission which was independently funded and allowed him to do more or less what he wanted in his territory, the Northern Peninsula and southern and central Labrador. He created a headquarters at St. Anthony, and in time a chain of hospitals and nursing stations stretched from North West River to White Bay. His example stimulated a public health movement in the colony focusing on the severe tuberculosis epidemic. Grenfell also started cooperatives and a sawmill, imported reindeer, and encouraged crafts and gardening. He was not greatly interested in the Native peoples of Labrador, who were left to missionaries and the Hudson's Bay Company. But he did stimulate interest in the territory, and a number of explorers investigated the interior, the most famous perhaps being the remarkable Mina Hubbard, who in 1905 trekked from North West River to Ungava Bay. More important was A.P. Low of the Canadian Geological Survey, who made a series of extraordinary journeys through the Labrador Peninsula in the 1890s and helped establish the territory's economic potential. Journeys like Low's caused increased interest in Labrador's forests by the early

Dr. Wilfred Grenfell leading a prayer meeting at the Grenfell mission in Battle Harbour, Labrador, 1914 (Maritime History Archives, Memorial University).

The Pink, White, and Green
The origins of this flag are obscure. One tradition holds that it descends from the flag of the Natives' Society, another that it was the creation of Bishop Fleming as a result of his intervention in disputes between sealers hauling wood for churches in St. John's. Recent research suggests that the flag appeared later in the nineteenth century, and was probably based on the colours of the Star of the Sea Association, a Roman Catholic fraternal society founded in 1871. The Pink, White, and Green was never an official flag, and certainly never republican.

twentieth century. Both Québec and Newfoundland claimed timber stands along the Grand or Hamilton River, and it was this dispute which sent the question of the definition of the interior boundary in 1907 to the Judicial Committee of the Privy Council in Britain.

Unlike Grenfell, Coaker was unknown outside Newfoundland. He chose to work within the system, his aim being to reform the fisheries and to ensure that the "toilers" (fishermen, sealers, loggers) received fair treatment from merchants and the government. The union established stores, a trading company, and a newspaper, lobbied the government energetically, and built a headquarters at Port Union in Trinity Bay. Coaker knew from the start that the FPU would have to enter politics in order to get the reforms it wanted, its programme laid out in the "Bonavista Platform" of 1912. Opposition from a conservative Roman Catholic hierarchy, which saw the FPU as dangerously socialistic, blunted the strength of Coaker's crusade. Nevertheless, he gained a devoted following along the northeast coast, and became a force to be reckoned with.

"Making fish at Turnavik," in Labrador during the 1890s (photo by Wilfred Grenfell, from *A History of Newfoundland*, by D.W. Prowse).

This was soon understood by Sir Edward Morris, who left the Bond government in 1907, formed his own People's Party (bankrolled by the Reids), and defeated the Liberals in 1909. Morris was a flexible politician, and would probably have accepted much of the FPU's programme had it not been necessary to maintain good relations with the Catholic Church and the equally anti-Coaker Board of Trade. Coaker became increasingly frustrated at Morris's inability to deliver what the FPU wanted, or to halt a wave of speculation in timber lands involving members of the government. He therefore threw his influence behind the Liberals.

Morris did give one gift to rural Newfoundland, however, as well as to the Reid Newfoundland Company. He announced a branch railway programme, and awarded the contracts to the Reids without tender. Before work ended in 1914, lines had been built to Bonavista, Trepassey, Grates Cove, and Heart's Content. They relentlessly lost money, and added significantly to the public debt. But they were popular, and no doubt helped Morris defeat the Liberal-FPU alliance in the 1913 general election.

Newfoundland entered the war in 1914 with enthusiasm and confidence, proud to be a member of the Empire, and proud of what had been achieved at home under responsible government. The century since the last major European war had seen many changes. Newfoundland was now a dominion; its economy had become more diversified; and its people, whatever their denomination or ancestry, were self-consciously Newfoundlanders, loyal to Britain, and self-characterized as tough, hardy, independent, and proud. The "First Five Hundred" of the Newfoundland Regiment which embarked on 4 October personified this sense of identity and nationalism. It was, however, an end as well as a beginning, since the war proved to be a watershed in the country's history.

Time Line

1815	End of the Napoleonic Wars.
1817	Governor stays year-round for the first time.
1819	Demasduit ("Mary March") captured and brought to St. John's.
1822	William Cormack walks across Newfoundland.
1823	Shawnadithit captured at Badger Bay with her mother and sister.
1824	Newfoundland becomes a Crown Colony.
1825	First highway opened, from St. John's to Portugal Cove.
1829	Death of Shawnadithit.
1832	Representative government granted, first elections.
1833	House of Assembly opens for the first time.
1836	First Education Act.
1846	Great fire in St. John's leaves 12,000 homeless.
1850	Colonial Building opens.
1855	Responsible government instituted; Liberal party forms government, led by P.F. Little.
1857	Census puts population at 122,638.
1862	Steamers used in the seal fishery for the first time.
1864	Establishment of Newfoundland Geological Survey; Tilt Cove copper mine opened.
1866	Transatlantic cable links Ireland and Heart's Content.
1869	Pro-confederates badly defeated in general election.
1871	Newfoundland Constabulary formed, a year after the withdrawal of British troops.
1878	First telephone system in St. John's.
1879	First successful daily newspaper: *The Evening Telegram*.
1881	Construction of the Newfoundland railway begins.
1883	Orange-Catholic affray at Harbour Grace.
1884	St. John's dry dock opens; census lists population at 197,589.

1885	Flavin Lane station produces the first electricity in St. John's.
1887	Secret ballot introduced.
1888	Municipal government in St. John's.
1890	Railway construction contract with R.G. Reid.
1892	8 July: Great Fire destroys much of downtown St. John's; Wilfred Grenfell's first voyage to Newfoundland and Labrador.
1893	Railway construction and operating contract with R.G. Reid.
1894	"Black Monday" (10 December): crash of the Union and Commercial banks.
1895	Canadian banks set up in St. John's; confederation negotiations fail; iron ore mining begins on Bell Island.
1897	Cornerstone of Cabot Tower laid.
1898	First train runs from St. John's to Port aux Basques; first pulp mill at Black River, Placentia Bay.
1901	12/13 December: Marconi receives the first transatlantic wireless signals at Signal Hill; formation of the Reid Newfoundland Company; population c. 220,000.
1902	Governor Cavendish Boyle composes "The Ode to Newfoundland."
1904	The *entente cordiale* ends French Shore dispute.
1905	Agreement with Anglo-Newfoundland Development Co. to build newsprint mill at Grand Falls.
1908	Tie election; foundation of the Fishermen's Protective Union.
1909	Branch line railway programme begins; Grand Falls mill opens; old age pensions introduced.
1914	Sealing disasters: the *Southern Cross* and the crew of the *Newfoundland*; outbreak of First World War, formation of the Newfoundland Regiment.

CHAPTER V

The Twentieth Century

Terry Bishop-Stirling and Jeff A. Webb

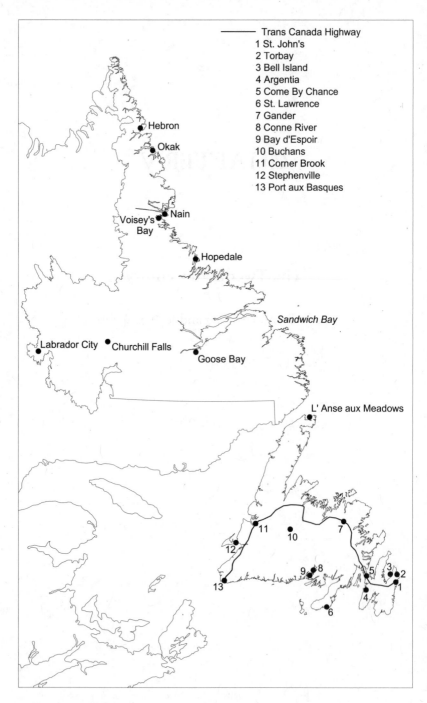

Major settlements of the twentieth century and the route of the Trans Canada Highway.

On the eve of the First World War, advances in transportation and communication had further weakened the "isolation" of Newfoundland and Labrador, an isolation never as complete as is often assumed. From 1914 to the end of the century, the country struggled to attain a North American lifestyle and level of consumption, while the economy remained based on the export of a few natural resources. Responding to a desire for "modernity," successive governments tried to diversify the economy and improve standards of communication, health, and education. But Newfoundlanders faced remarkable challenges, ranging from economic and natural disasters to two world wars. They started the century as residents of a self-governing colony and moved through a "benevolent dictatorship" to become citizens of Canada's youngest province. The efforts to modernize were not always successful, and had costs as well as benefits. Through it all, people preserved their dynamic culture and identity. Newfoundland and Labrador's talented artists, actors, musicians, scholars, and writers reflected and reinforced its people's resilience, humour, and continued hope for the future.

The First World War and Its Aftermath

When Britain declared war in 1914, Newfoundland immediately pledged its support. While Newfoundlanders debated the exact nature of our participation, most citizens approved of Prime Minister Morris's decision to raise a Newfoundland regiment. Morris resisted suggestions that he form a coalition government, appointing a non-partisan volunteer committee to direct the war effort. The Newfoundland Patriotic Association (NPA), under the leadership of Governor Davidson, included politicians from all parties, leading businessmen, and professionals. The NPA directed recruitment, appointed officers, and arranged the training and transportation of servicemen.

More than 12,000 Newfoundland men served in uniform, mostly in either the British or Canadian forces. Others were willing to go overseas but failed to meet the medical standards, a reflection of the state of nutrition prevailing at the beginning of the century. Initially, a larger portion of people in St. John's enlisted than from the outports, where the labour of young sons was needed to haul the cod traps if families were to prosper. Many of the first 500 to enlist had been members of the military-style St. John's youth groups such as the Church Lads Brigade. In other parts of the empire, first-generation British immigrants were quick to sign up, bolstering their enlistment statistics. But since 98.6 per cent of its population was native-born, the number of Newfoundland volunteers cannot be easily compared to those of a country such as Canada.

Women also supported the war effort. Nurses signed up to serve in convalescent hospitals and at the front. They were joined by members of the

A First World War army training camp in Pleasantville (Archives and Manuscripts, Memorial University Library).

Voluntary Aid Detachment, who were given a few weeks of first aid training and were soon providing basic care under the guidance of the nursing sisters. At home, the Women's Patriotic Association (WPA) provided comforts such as extra food and clothing to soldiers, visited families of men on the casualty list, provided entertainment and supplementary health care for servicemen, and supported the recruitment efforts of the NPA. By the end of the war, women in close to 300 communities had built a colony-wide organization which produced over 62,000 pairs of socks, ran a convalescent hospital for returned men, and raised funds for women and children in devastated European countries.

For those who remained at home, the war brought several changes. Newfoundland's resource industries boomed as European production declined. Workers benefited as Newfoundland experienced labour shortages, but these benefits were largely offset by inflation. By 1917, widespread rumours of war profiteering, devastating losses overseas, and good economic opportunities at home combined to slow recruitment to a trickle. Facing an upcoming election, Morris appointed a commission to investigate wartime profits, and began negotiating a coalition with opposition parties. In July 1917, the leaders of all parties formed a National Government.

Many Newfoundlanders were proud that the country had its own regiment in the British Army, though some people, in the outports in particular, favoured expanding the Royal Naval Reserve and providing the Royal Navy with experienced seamen. A significant number of outport men enlisted in the navy, serving on the ships that kept the sea lanes safe for British merchant traffic. The Newfoundland Regiment fought with distinction at Gallipoli before being transferred to France. Its sacrifice in the Battle of the Somme

The Red Cross Committee of the Women's Patriotic Association, at Government House (The Rooms Provincial Archives).

stood out in particular. Near the village of Beaumont Hamel, on 1 July 1916, 753 men marched into the German machine gun fire, leaving only sixty-eight able to answer roll call the next day. About one-third of the Regiment had been held in reserve in Great Britain, and, once reinforced with more recruits, it went on to fight in several more significant battles, including Monchy-le-Preaux, Ypres, and Cambrai. In recognition of its role in these latter two battles, the Regiment was awarded the title "Royal," the only regiment given this honour during the First World War.

The magnitude of the Colony's losses on 1 July devastated many families, leaving everyone feeling that young men who would have done great things had died that day. The sense of unfulfilled promise and the fact that no St. John's neighbourhood or Newfoundland community was untouched led subsequent generations to believe that Newfoundland's losses had been greater than that of any other country. A historian cannot easily compare Newfoundland's casualty rates with those of other countries because the scale is so different. If he or she compares the losses of the Newfoundland Regiment with other battalions of the same size, there were regiments which had greater casualties. Yet Newfoundland's casualties were among the highest in the empire. Furthermore, perhaps no country had a regiment which so closely represented the nation as a whole, and which lost so many men in a single morning. People would not soon forget the image of those men tucking their chins into their collars as if they were facing a hailstorm and purposefully walking into the machine gun fire.

The heavy losses had convinced many people, especially those in St. John's, that conscription was necessary if the country were to maintain a separate regiment. William Coaker, as a member of the cabinet, defended

British Navy ships at anchor in St. John's harbour during the First World War.

compulsory service, which most FPU members opposed, by arguing that he would now be in a position to ensure that the war's costs would be shared more evenly. Responding to the Cost of Living Commission's report on wartime profiteering, the new government created a Board of Food Control and implemented a war profits tax and a modest income tax. It also created a Militia Department, which took over direction of the war effort from the NPA, and enacted long-overdue legislation, providing servicemen with death benefits and disability pensions. Conscription was delayed for one last-ditch recruitment campaign, but was finally enacted in April 1918. The act was unpopular in outport Newfoundland, where many argued that the small colony had done enough and should now focus on feeding the allies. The war ended before any conscripts made it to the front, but long-term damage had been done to relations between the capital and the outports, to Coaker's credibility, and to the unity of the FPU.

In 1918 the people of Newfoundland and Labrador celebrated peace and welcomed home the men and women who had served overseas. Tragically, even the long-awaited reunions were accompanied by more sorrow as some returning veterans carried the deadly Spanish flu. As elsewhere, the government and doctors were helpless in the face of the deadly and fast-spreading virus. The flu appeared first in St. John's in October 1918 and quickly spread to the outports; by November it had reached Labrador. In an effort to halt contagion, the government closed churches, theatres, and other public meeting places and banned meetings of more than twelve people. In the capital, the Seamen's Institute was hastily converted to a hospital and in nine weeks provided 3,521 days of care for 267 patients; thirty-two of these flu victims died. The approximately seventy doctors practicing outside St. John's tried to serve their own patients and raced from community to community, responding to desperate telegraphs requesting help. In Labrador, the situation was even worse. By January 1919, seventy out of 320 people had died in Sandwich Bay. A February report from Hopedale described a rapidly deteriorating situation in Hebron and Okak. Both communities were essentially wiped out by flu: Hebron, with a population of approximately 100, suffered eighty-four deaths in a ten-day period in November. In the end, the Inuit population had fallen by one-third, from an estimated 1,270 to 875. Before it ran its course, the disease would take at least 232 lives on the island and twice as many in Labrador.

Later generations would look upon the war years with mixed feelings. Newfoundland seemed to have earned a place of respect among larger nations in the midst of the carnage, but the war and the flu had taken a great toll. Like veterans and civilians elsewhere, people in Newfoundland and Labrador hoped the sacrifices made would bring lasting peace, and greater justice and prosperity. The country's war effort was recognized with honours to individuals; pride was evident in the more frequent use of the term Dominion and in support for post-war memorials. However, the long-term economic impact of the war was devastating, and, throughout the 1920s, successive governments struggled to meet both old and new financial responsibilities.

Search for Stability in the 1920s

By early 1919 open partisan politics resumed, with each political party being either a loose coalition of like-minded people, or followers of an influential leader. Parties changed frequently as the principal actors jockeyed for power, so party names are not a perfect guide to political philosophy. The Tories, however, tended to be supported by workers in St. John's whose livelihood depended upon manufacturing and by the business class, especially those who wanted little government interference in the fishery. Liberals, and the FPU's Union Party, portrayed themselves as champions of outport fishermen and loggers, while also arguing for industrial development of land resources.

Changing relationships within the empire led the British government to pass the Statute of Westminster, which recognized some former colonies as self-governing Dominions. Newfoundland adopted the title of Dominion around 1918, but the Newfoundland legislature was one of the Dominions which chose not to assume all the rights listed in the Statute of Westminster of 1931. For example, Newfoundland continued to have Great Britain negotiate with other countries on its behalf. The end of the war prompted a world-wide economic recession, and the government was preoccupied with finding money to support the payments on the national debt. The $16 million debt from paying for the regiment now added to loans taken on for building and operating the railway, so assuming new international responsibilities seemed premature.

High wartime prices for fish and paper had masked deep structural weaknesses in the economy. In 1921, interest on wartime debts, combined

Opening of the War Memorial, 1 July 1924 (Archives and Manuscripts, Memorial University Library).

with new obligations to veterans and their families, had added $1.75 million to the country's annual expenditure. This figure represented approximately half the average annual expenditure for the five years preceding the war. Without significant post-war economic growth, the debt would threaten Newfoundland's future. This growth did not materialize and in the 1920s governments met rising economic costs with continued borrowing.

Newfoundland fish exporters continued to face problems of quality, marketing, and increased international competition, which had been evident in the industry from the late 1880s. The Union Party, the political arm of the FPU, formed a coalition with a revived Liberal-Reform party under Squires. When this coalition came to power in November 1919, Coaker became Minister of Marine and Fisheries. He now had the opportunity to implement a series of fishery regulations designed to improve quality and ensure the more efficient marketing practices that the FPU had long sought. By January 1921 these regulations had failed. Several fish exporters refused to cooperate with a government that meddled in their business, and there were weak penalties for those who evaded the cooperative marketing rules. The opposition party and many merchants could not overcome their antipathy toward Coaker and the FPU, even if some of the regulations were good for the industry. Even without local opposition, problems in the international banking sector and market conditions had not made it a favourable time to introduce such a bold reorganization.

Between 1920 and 1923, Newfoundland, like much of the western world, continued to experience economic problems created by the post-war disruption in trade. Most government revenue came from customs duties on imported goods, products which could only be paid for with exports of pulp and paper, minerals, and fish. As exports slumped, many merchants hesitated

A lumber camp in White Bay, 1924 (Newfoundland Historical Society).

to advance credit to the clients who were unable to pay off the full balance of what was owed, and a large portion of fishing and logging families faced hard times. With fewer imports, government revenue fell at the same time that people needed public relief while they waited for exports to revive. A government surplus of $1,350,556 in 1919-1920 was followed by a deficit of over $4 million the next year. The depression caused layoffs at the paper mill at Grand Falls and the Bell Island iron ore mine. Problems in the resource sector also led to business failures in wholesale and retail enterprises and factories in St. John's. Throughout the colony 242 businesses failed between 1921 and 1923. By 1921 there were 10,000 unemployed and many fishing families were unable to get additional credit from their merchants, leading to widespread demands for government aid. Between 1908 and 1913 able-bodied relief had cost the treasury an average of $7,039; from 1920 to 1924 this figure rose to $794,549. Able-bodied relief never fell below $100,000 annually through the rest of the 1920s. During the spring of 1921 some of the unemployed in St. John's formed a committee, and labour unrest was almost continuous. In some outports fishermen threatened to march on the capital. The government used its own police force and timely visits from British warships to try to control unrest. It also implemented make-work projects to relieve stress without promoting pauperism, a term reflecting the fear that government "handouts" would sap working people's willingness to help themselves. In the spring of 1922 the government borrowed $500,000 to advance fishing supplies to planters through local merchants. While this met with general support, other forms of make-work projects were less popular and were later judged expensive, inefficient, and poorly administered.

Despite their economic concerns, people also wanted to honour another debt—to those who had lost their lives during the war. They debated the appropriate form of memorials: some favoured a stone and brass monument, while others wanted more of a living memorial. In the end the country did both, building a national war monument in St. John's, erecting memorials at each of the sites of significant battle in Europe, and creating Memorial University College, which would train teachers and start young Newfoundlanders working toward higher education. Many leaders believed that the sectarian divisions of the school system should not be reproduced in post-secondary education. Just as Roman Catholic and Protestant men had fought side by side, now they would sit side by side in the classroom.

Another hopeful development in this otherwise bleak economic period was the granting of timber rights to British industrialists to construct a second paper mill at Corner Brook on the island's west coast. Despite having been a long-time opponent of the project, Squires took credit for this modern industry. Squires's industrial policy and his skilful partisan manoeuvring had won him election in May 1923 but made him enemies among the Tories. When theft within his administration came to light, Squires resigned when faced with a revolt by his cabinet. William Warren formed a government, and to deal with the political scandal appointed a British barrister, Thomas Hollis Walker, to investigate. Hollis Walker found a number of financial irregularities, and the publication of his damning report convinced many voters that Newfoundland politicians were corrupt. The resulting widespread cynicism about politics lingered through the decade. In the wake of the political turmoil following Squires's fall, Newfoundland went through three short-lived administrations before a general election in 1924 saw the assumption of power by a conservative St. John's-dominated party. Led by businessman Walter Monroe, the new government promised "to clean up, keep clean, and to give stable government."

During the First World War, suffrage leaders had postponed their demands, but now resumed their fight for the right to vote. Arguing that women as contributing citizens deserved the franchise, the new suffrage group sought to include women from all regions, classes, and religions. Through public debates, speeches, and letters to newspapers, the suffragists attempted to convert the public and politicians to their cause. Many suffragists had joined the executive of the WPA and had supported the war effort, and this won them supporters among the leading newspapers, political leaders, and war veterans. Public opinion strongly favoured women's suffrage, but the post-war recession and the intransigence of Squires disappointed suffragists. In 1921, responding to Squires's suggestion that they did not represent most

A wedding party at Old Glory Hall on Topsail Road, St. John's, c. 1930s (Archives and Manuscripts, Memorial University Library).

Newfoundland women, the newly formed Women's Franchise League used the WPA network to circulate a petition throughout the country, obtaining some 10,000 names. In the 1924 election campaign both major parties promised to pass a suffrage bill and, when elected, the Conservatives under Walter Monroe fulfilled their promise. The Election Act of 1925 gave women the right to vote once they were twenty-five years of age, while men only had to be twenty-one. Women could also sit as members of the House of Assembly. Three women ran in the next municipal election in 1925 and in the next colonial election in 1928 an estimated 90 per cent of women voted. The first woman to be elected to the Assembly was Helena Squires, who won a by-election in 1930. Ironically, Squires was the wife of the suffragists' leading opponent.

Monroe's merchant-backed party came to power as the international trade recession eased and as the positive effects of the pulp and paper mill at Corner Brook began to be felt: The colony was also buoyed in 1927 when the Judicial Committee of the British Privy Council decided the long-running Labrador Boundary dispute between Canada and Newfoundland in the latter's favour. The coast of Labrador had been assigned to Newfoundland, so the case hinged upon the meaning of the word "coast." The Canadian position was that Newfoundland had jurisdiction over a thin ribbon of land running along the sea shore, but the court decided that all the land with rivers flowing into the sea belonged to Newfoundland.

This confirmed Newfoundland control over a vast territory with a wealth of untapped natural resources. The Inuit and Innu were not consulted, but

Boys rolling barrels to the Hopedale Mission, in 1938. Started by the Moravians, the Labrador mission was taken over by Wilfred Grenfell (The Rooms Provincial Archives).

settlers of European descent gave depositions. Despite the court decision, Newfoundland's economic recovery was limited. Monroe was unable to end "reckless" relief spending and further borrowing because economic conditions remained poor. In four years the government added $17 million to the public debt.

Early in his mandate Monroe enacted popular legislation such as the repeal of prohibition (which had been adopted during the war), but was soon criticized for blatantly class-biased taxation policies. Within six months of taking office, his government repealed the income tax, which few working-class Newfoundlanders paid, and increased tariffs on goods such as tobacco, rope, twine, fishing nets, and margarine. The opposition argued that these increases imposed higher prices on already over-burdened outport consumers, but the government defended the duties as an attempt to protect manufacturing and local jobs in St. John's. The growing discontent with Monroe's administration made way for Squires's return to power in 1928, as his party successfully presented itself as the champion of the outport working man.

Men continued to leave their homes for weeks at a time for the bank fishery, and longer periods for the Labrador floater fishery. Sometimes whole families relocated from the island to Labrador for the summer. Life in inshore fishing communities continued to have much the same rhythm it had had for a century. Men went to the fishing grounds each morning, returning in

Riots of 1932 (The Rooms Provincial Archives).

the afternoon to split and salt their catch. Women tended to their gardens and the children while keeping an eye on the drying fish, which they turned frequently and protected from the rain. There had been changes, however: not all men had to row to and from their nets or cod traps as two-stroke engines were becoming common. Motor boats also encouraged a further division of income; families who could afford cod traps and motors were able to employ men who could afford neither. Since families had to pay for expensive gear, they needed to catch greater volumes of fish to pay for their capital investment. As some fish companies started to experiment in freezing fish rather than salting it, people became trapped in a cycle of needing more fish to pay for new gear and needing new gear to be able to catch more fish. In the long run, even though fish was being overharvested, governments, exporters, and fish harvesters were powerless to reduce pressure upon the resource.

The Depression and the Loss of Democracy

If people felt that the next new technology, or better marketing, could put the fishery on a sound footing, such optimism was impossible to sustain after 1929. The second Squires government soon had to cope with the Great Depression, a world-wide economic phenomenon which hit the small export-dependant Newfoundland very hard. In April 1932 another series of financial scandals, combined with the severe hardship of the unemployed, led to a riot at the legislature, from which Squires barely escaped with his life. Frederick Alderdice was elected on a campaign to govern well and a promise to ask the British government to consider whether responsible government should be suspended and the country governed by a commission. Nevertheless, Alderdice sought alternatives to this drastic constitutional change. He cut expenditures to the bone, submitted to increasingly strict control over government finances

Sailors playing cards in between convoy duties, St. John's (courtesy of Library and Archives Canada).

by representatives of the country's creditors, and suggested to the British that Newfoundland reschedule its debt payments at a lower rate of interest. The government in London did not want a dominion of the British Empire to default, but did not believe that the British taxpayers would accept bailing out the Newfoundland government unless the British Treasury had control over how the money was spent. The British Government appointed a Royal Commission led by Lord Amulree to investigate conditions in Newfoundland. Britain hoped that Canada would take responsibility for Newfoundland, but once it became clear that Canada was struggling with its own financial crisis, the British Government decided to suspend the constitution.

Instead of finding economic factors at the root of the country's financial crisis, Amulree blamed democracy. Most Newfoundlanders were relieved to have British financial aid and were willing to have the constitution suspended. Amulree convinced the Newfoundland prime minister to accept the recommendations and have the Newfoundland government vote itself out of existence without holding an election on the question, as Alderdice had earlier promised. The British indicated that when Newfoundland was again self-supporting, and, if Newfoundlanders asked for a resumption of responsible government, the previous constitution would be restored. In February 1934 a new government consisting of six appointees and the governor as chairman was sworn in. The three British commissioners took responsibility for the areas of financial reconstruction and economic development—Finance, Natural Resources, and Public Utilities. The Newfoundland-born commissioners administered Health and Welfare, Justice, and Home Affairs and Education. No one imagined at the time that the Commission of Government would last until 1949.

The advent of Commission of Government was initially met with quiet acceptance as people hoped for relief and leadership to help them rebuild their country. Such high hopes, perhaps unrealistic, were soon dashed as the Commission proved unable to bring about economic recovery. Despite the Commission's continued lectures on self-reliance and the dangers of pauperization, large segments of the unemployed and the working poor faced real privation. While it is true that rural families could generally provide more of their food than could urban ones, not all areas of Newfoundland and Labrador had the agricultural capabilities that politicians and some social reformers assumed. Like its democratic predecessors, the government fell back on providing able-bodied relief and support to volunteer philanthropic groups who aided the poor. In keeping with Amulree's judgement that Newfoundlanders' "moral fibre" and work ethic had been weakened, the new government instructed relief officers to ensure that people received the dole only when they had exhausted all means of support. Individuals who met these requirements were given monthly relief vouchers valued at $1.80 per person. These vouchers could be redeemed with the local relief merchant for a limited range of basic foodstuffs, including the nutritious but despised brown, "dole flour." Since few non-food items could be obtained with the allowance, inadequate clothing and the absence of "luxuries" such as books and tobacco added to the misery of the poor. The resources of philanthropic organizations were spread thin as they tried to respond to increasing need. In St. John's, for example, the Child Welfare Association added soup kitchens to its existing programmes of health education and services for children. By the end of the 1930s the Commission was unpopular, especially after the government approved the sale of the Corner Brook Mill to Bowater in 1938, thus abandoning the prospect of a third paper mill. The growing dissent caused the Commissioners to worry that Newfoundlanders might demand a return to responsible government, even though government finances were not yet secure.

The Commission improved health care in much of Newfoundland, while leaving Labrador and the most northern parts of the island to the hospitals and nursing stations of the International Grenfell Association. By 1938 more than forty district nurses had been hired to work throughout the colony, and outside the capital over half of the physicians were on government salary. The General Hospital and the tuberculosis sanatorium in St. John's were both expanded, and from 1934 to 1938 ten cottage hospitals were built in outports, providing 130 beds for patients. Medical insurance offered many people care at these new facilities. For $2.50 per year, a family was entitled to treatment, and payment was accepted in cash, goods, or labour. The 12,800 residents of the south coast from Fortune Bay to Port aux Basques received health services and treatment from the hospital ship the *Lady Anderson*. The Commission also promoted preventative health through a widespread education programme. The Avalon Health Unit provided a travelling x-ray service to detect tuberculosis and the colony's first diagnostic laboratory opened in 1935.

Marian Wingate and Margaret Little of WRCNS at work in St. John's (courtesy of Library and Archives Canada).

Despite being an honest and efficient government, the Commission failed to solve the country's underlying economic problems. The average number of monthly relief recipients had increased from 31,899 in 1934 to 38,187 in 1939. The health care services were welcome, but major improvements in people's health required improvement in the economy. In 1940, ninety-one of every 1,000 children still died in their first year of life and the tuberculosis rate was thirty-four times higher than in Canada. Without world-wide economic recovery, it would be unrealistic to expect the Commission to have eradicated tuberculosis or to have significantly lowered infant mortality rates in just fifteen years. But the Commission was also hampered by its contradictory goals: lowering expenditure to balance the budget and increasing spending to address social and economic needs. The Commission's health care programme was undermined by its meagre relief rations, which did not assure the poor the adequate food, clothing, and shelter needed to maintain health.

Amulree had accurately described conditions in 1933, but since he had wrongly diagnosed that political incompetence and moral weakness were responsible for the country's difficulties, the cure of a "rest from politics" did little to ease the hardship of the Great Depression. The Commission tried to develop a land settlement scheme, moving some of the unemployed to areas where they could farm. It hoped to take pressure off relief rolls, and that the individualism of Newfoundlanders would be replaced by a spirit of cooperation. Between 1934 and 1938, the Commission invested over $800,000 in five such settlements, farmed by 171 families. The settlements never became financially self-supporting and a 1938 report by a British expert criticized the scheme as wasteful and poorly planned. The failure of the land settlements shook faith in the Commission and discouraged future experiments. In a related initiative, the Government encouraged the growth of cooperatives, hoping that producers banding together could break the influence of the fish

The Second World War brought thousands of Canadian and American armed forces personnel to Newfoundland and Labrador. Large air bases were built at several locations, including St. John's, Argentia, Gander, Stephenville, and Goose Bay (shown here during the war) (The Rooms Provincial Archives).

merchant and improve everyone's living standards. The cooperative rhetoric raised accusations that the Commission was encouraging class warfare. Once the Second World War started, the government quietly abandoned both land settlements and cooperative initiatives as it attempted to balance the budget and end borrowing from British development funds.

While many families experienced hardship during the Great Depression, it was also a period of cultural revival. Several foreign folksong collectors visited Newfoundland to collect ballads and music, and some Newfoundlanders participated in the international movement to preserve folksongs. Patent medicine distributor Gerald S. Doyle, for example, collected songs which he published in a booklet he distributed free to advertise his products. This songbook and his radio programme, the *Gerald S. Doyle News Bulletin*, reflected a renewed interest in Newfoundland culture and national life despite the hardship and absence of an elected government. Similarly, journalist Joseph Smallwood published several works of history and politics, including the first two volumes of the *Book of Newfoundland*, a compendium of essays. Smallwood also created a nationalistic radio programme, the *Barrelman*, which provided him with a venue to encourage patriotism and confidence at a time when things looked very bleak.

The War and Economic Recovery

When Germany invaded Poland in 1939, Newfoundland, as part of the empire, was at war. This time no one proposed an infantry regiment, perhaps feeling that the sacrifice during the first war had been too great for the small

Were We Poor Before Confederation?

Many of those who feel Confederation was the right choice, and who welcome the concrete benefits of Canadian social programmes, remember the widespread poverty in parts of the country. Others believe that Smallwood exaggerated poverty to make it seem that confederation rescued people from a dismal life, but do not deny that there was both poverty and wealth. A few claim that most people thrived during the Depression and blame the post-confederation endemic unemployment and low standards of living upon the Canadian welfare state. They argue that social programmes encouraged a culture of dependence. None of these perspectives tell the whole story.

Certainly, for many who voted in 1948, "a return to responsible government as it existed in 1933" raised memories of deprivation and a humiliating dependence on relief. Other families had done well, managing to remain self-supporting and even prosper. Some people had little money but did not go without food, while other families experienced hunger and nutritional diseases. How one fared depended upon the locally available resources, how many sons and daughters there were who were old enough to contribute to the family income, and many other factors.

Joseph R. Smallwood (Clara [Russell] Smallwood Collection).

In the National Convention, Smallwood had compared the rates of nutritional diseases in Newfoundland with other North American jurisdictions, and argued that we were especially poor. Such comparisons are tricky. Some areas of North America with similar rural populations likely had comparable health statistics, so we have to ensure we are comparing like units when making statements such as "Newfoundland had the highest rate of beri-beri in North America."

Newfoundland's finances were stable at the time of confederation. Canada did not inherit a bankrupt and desperate province in 1949. The colony was able to meet its debt payments and, thanks to its wartime prosperity, had accumulated a financial surplus. The federal government took over most of Newfoundland's long-term debt and liabilities such as operating the railway, as it had done for the other colonies that had joined the union. Some subsequent commentators pointed out that Newfoundland's 1948 debt was less than the per capita debt of Canada, a debt Newfoundlanders now shared. It must be remembered that Newfoundland's per capita income, and thus its ability to handle that debt, was much lower than Canada's. Arguments comparing debt burdens must therefore be approached with caution.

What could not be known in 1948 was the economic future of an independent Newfoundland. Confederates argued that current good times were solely the result of artificial wartime conditions, while responsible government advocates stressed the country's rich resources. Voters weighed these arguments based on their own experiences and prospects. By a small majority, they chose the security of union with Canada and the guarantees of family allowances and old age pensions over the uncertainties of an independent Newfoundland.

nation. More than 12,000 Newfoundlanders were engaged in the war effort, about the same number of people who had participated in the First World War. The British Army designated two Royal Artillery regiments as Newfoundland units and the recruiting propaganda encouraged enlistment to maintain the Newfoundland character of those units. Many Newfoundlanders also served in the Royal Navy, the Royal Air Force, and in each of the branches of the Canadian armed services. Over 500 Newfoundland women enlisted in the women's branches of the Canadian Army, Royal Canadian Navy, and Royal Canadian Air Force. Newfoundland loggers also served in the Overseas Forestry Unit, which cut timber in Scotland for use as props to hold up coal mines. Although they wore no uniform, many who faced the toughest conditions and the greatest risks of death were those who served on merchant vessels, keeping the allies supplied with food and war matériel from North America. The merchant marine accounted for 257 of the approximately 900 deaths of Newfoundlanders serving in the Second World War. Closer to home, over 200 people were killed in German submarine attacks on the Gulf ferry SS *Caribou*, and in two separate attacks on iron ore carriers in Conception Bay.

Canada took responsibility for the defence of Newfoundland, taking over air facilities at Gander, building new airfields at Torbay and Goose Bay, and operating a naval base in St. John's. The Canadians were joined by thousands of Americans after Great Britain and the United States signed the destroyers-for-bases deal, well before the Americans entered the war. Starting in 1941 the Americans built an army base in St. John's, an airfield in Stephenville, and a naval base in Argentia. Both the Canadians and Americans also operated small weather stations, radar posts, and other specialized facilities. By the end of the war Canadians had spent an estimated $100 million in Newfoundland and Labrador, and Americans had invested at least three times that amount. By late 1941, the bases became a major impetus to economic growth. At its peak, base construction employed an estimated 10,000 Newfoundlanders and thereafter provided jobs for approximately 5,000 civilian men and women. Government revenue reached an unprecedented $33.3 million in 1944-1945. During the war years the country collected $32.5 million more than it spent. Some of this revenue was used to expand public services, while $12.3 million was granted to Britain in interest-free loans. Some Newfoundlanders thought the money should be spent in Newfoundland rather than lent to the British. Others thought the wartime windfall should be used to pay down the debt, which had been accumulating over the preceding decades.

Newfoundland's resource industries flourished during the conflict as well. Fish prices rose from $4.50 a quintal in 1938 to $10.50 in 1942, and lumber and iron ore prices also skyrocketed as producers tried to meet the demand brought on by the war. Increased markets for food also encouraged entrepreneurs who were beginning to develop a fresh-frozen fishing industry in

Newfoundland. Higher consumer income also benefited local manufacturers and wholesale and retail businesses. Canadian and American employers also recruited at least 3,600 Newfoundlanders to meet labour shortages in their countries, while during the Depression Newfoundlanders had difficulty going to either country in search of work. For many Newfoundlanders, wartime conditions provided regular cash wages for the first time. Local employers struggled to retain workers, prompting the Commission to ask the Americans to keep wages in base construction low enough that other industries could afford to hire workers. This encouraged resentment of the Commission. The availability of wage-paying jobs also accelerated a pre-war trend away from the credit system; a 1944 law enforcing payment in cash likely reflected and reinforced a change created by the labour market.

The "friendly invasion" of thousands of young Canadian and American servicemen changed more than the economy of Newfoundland. The WPA re-formed and together with other women's groups supported the war effort by providing comforts for men overseas, running hospitality facilities, and entertaining troops at the regular dances held in St. John's. Newfoundland women also obtained good jobs, often for the first time. As well as serving in the military, women worked as clerks and domestics on the bases, or obtained employment in the rapidly expanding service and retail sectors. Thousands of Newfoundland girls married their Canadian and American sweethearts; many others were left heartbroken, often with children to raise alone.

The visiting troops brought their culture with them through their manners, customs, and tastes. Newfoundlanders were long familiar with American movies, magazines, and radio, but now they had closer contact with Americans. Stars such as Bob Hope and Frank Sinatra visited troops in Newfoundland, and the US radio station VOUS from Fort Pepperrell reached civilians with American popular music, comedy, and drama. This increased exposure to North American culture during the war again hastened the pre-war trends of embracing American popular culture and emulating their lifestyle.

Debating Newfoundland's Future

In 1943 the Commission changed the tax code to raise more money which could be used to contribute to the war effort. This encouraged many, including the influential Board of Trade, which represented the St. John's business community, to demand a return to elected government. Despite having set aside some money during the war, the Dominions Office decided that it would take a significant financial investment in Newfoundland to make the county self-supporting, money that the British Treasury would not approve. Meanwhile some Canadian officials had come to believe that having Newfoundland join the confederation would be in the best interest of Canada. The Dominions Office accepted that position and wanted to create the conditions whereby Newfoundlanders would ask to join the Canadian confederation. The Canadians were concerned that Newfoundland might develop closer relations with the United States and that the country's resources and strategic location might benefit the US. To give Newfoundlanders the opportunity to ask for union with Canada, the British created a National Convention to which voters in each of the old districts could elect representatives. The Convention would examine the economic conditions and recommend forms of government, among which voters would choose in a forthcoming referendum. The British, however, retained final say as to what choices would appear on the ballot. Nightly radio broadcasts of the Convention allowed listeners to follow the debate about Newfoundland's political future. A few Convention members, including Joseph Smallwood, favoured confederation over a return to responsible government. The majority of members, however, wanted to remain a self-governing colony, or thought that responsible government status should resume and then an elected government could negotiate union with Canada if it chose to.

In 1948 a delegation of the Convention travelled to Ottawa where the Canadian government offered terms of union, and, upon returning to St. John's, Smallwood used the broadcasts to inform voters of the material benefits of confederation. The anti-confederates had not worried about this. They thought, that since they had a majority in the Convention, they could keep confederation off the ballot in the forthcoming referendum. Advocates for responsible government had miscalculated: the British had long intended to have confederation on the ballot. In the first of two referenda on 3 June, 41.4 per cent voted for confederation, 44.5 per cent for responsible government, and 14.3 per cent for continuation of the Commission. Since no choice had a majority, the Commission option was dropped, and a second referendum was held on 22 July. The campaign now took an unfortunate turn when long-standing prejudices were reawakened and the campaign became sectarian and nasty. An anti-confederate editorial in the Roman Catholic newspaper the *Monitor* enabled the confederates to unfairly portray the Catholic Church as attempting to dominate politics. In the end, 52.3 per cent voted for confederation and 47.6 per cent for responsible government. Historians have debated the regional, class, sectarian, and other factors that influenced the geographic pattern of the vote. Of those living on the Avalon Peninsula 67.3 per cent had cast their ballot for responsible government, while on the rest of the island and in Labrador this option only garnered 31.9 per cent. A slim majority had chosen the social safety net of Canada over the risks of a return to responsible government as it existed in 1933.

The Commission appointed a group of Newfoundlanders to negotiate terms of union between Canada and Newfoundland, but there was little room for substantive negotiation since the federal and provincial areas of responsibility had been set out in the British North America Act of 1867. Control over the fisheries, for example, was a federal power. As had happened

The Newfoundland government conducted an extensive campaign to eliminate tuberculosis after the Second World War, using ships and buses as testing facilities. This photograph was taken at Memorial University in the mid-1960s (Archives and Manuscripts, Memorial University Library).

when the other colonies joined Canada, the federal government took over the majority of Newfoundland's public debt and the ownership of some assets such as the railway. The provincial government retained the surplus that the Commission had accumulated, and was to use it to improve public services and foster economic development. The people of the province elected seven Members of Parliament, and they had some influence in setting federal policy, but the province was left with very expensive areas of jurisdiction, including education, health, and social services. Newfoundland no longer collected customs revenue or income tax after 1949 so, like other provinces, it depended upon fiscal transfers from the Government of Canada. The anti-confederates had warned that the provincial government would be unable to pay for the level of services that people expected, so the federal government agreed to an extra grant to Newfoundland for the first eight years of confederation. When the eight years was up, a Royal Commission set the level of support. The province faced having a large portion of its revenue come from Ottawa and yet remained unable to balance its budget.

Was Confederation a Conspiracy?

Many of those who fought for the return of responsible government felt that the process by which Newfoundland entered Canada was flawed. Given that Confederation has not lived up to the promises Smallwood made during the Confederation debates, some people look back at the process with skepticism. The anti-confederates of the 1940s believed, rightly as it turned out, that the British and the Canadian governments were not neutral

Telephone dial-up service began in Newfoundland in 1948. By the mid-1970s Newfoundland Telephone Company Limited had installed computerized switches in the St. John's region (The Rooms Provincial Archives).

bystanders, but wanted Newfoundland to become a province. Both these governments did what they could to encourage Newfoundlanders to join Canada, but the ultimate decision was in the hands of Newfoundland voters. The anti-confederates held a majority in the National Convention, so they believed that their vote to omit confederation from the ballot should prevail. But many Newfoundlanders wanted confederation, arguing that they should have been denied the opportunity to vote for union with Canada does not seem democratic.

A few conspiracy-minded people suggest that the government told Smallwood to move to Gander in 1943 to make it easier for him to get elected, that it was his decision to carry the National Convention debates on the radio so that he, a former broadcaster, would have an advantage. But Smallwood moved long before the government decided to create a convention and the Broadcasting Corporation of Newfoundland, not the British Government, decided to broadcast the Convention.

Other people have suggested that Newfoundland should have been allowed to negotiate "Economic Union" with the United States. The Commission was self-serving in not allowing the Convention to discuss trade with the US, but the Economic Union Association's hope that free trade would make Newfoundland prosper under responsible government was unrealistic. The

Americans had what they wanted, ninety-nine-year leases for their bases. Newfoundlanders had long hoped to sell products to the US duty-free, but the Americans would not have granted Newfoundland preferential trade status when it needed the cooperation of Iceland and Norway during the Cold War. Furthermore, the US accepted that Newfoundland was part of the British Empire, and had no intention of interfering in its political process.

While no one in 1948 asked for a re-count or suggested the referendum had been unfair, years later stories surfaced that the referendum had been rigged. In the absence of any evidence of fraud, we must assume that indeed a majority of people voted for union with Canada.

Some of the people who supported responsible government were not opposed to confederation; they believed that Newfoundland should have returned to responsible government first, at which point an elected Newfoundland government could have negotiated union. The British and Canadians wanted to avoid this, fearing that the Newfoundlanders would drive such a hard bargain that union would be unacceptable to other provinces whose deal within confederation would be weaker by comparison. Getting back responsible government first makes some sense; people would have had the pride of negotiating on an equal footing rather than feeling that Newfoundland went to Ottawa with cap in hand. But the eventual terms of union would have been largely the same either way; political reality was that the division of powers was set in the British North America Act of 1867 and Newfoundland could not have been given something which was not given to other provinces.

In the end, some people remained unhappy about the process by which Newfoundland had entered Canada. When confederation failed to live up to people's expectations, some Newfoundlanders and Labradorians felt we had sold ourselves to Canada too cheaply. Pro-confederates in Canada helped to finance Smallwood's campaign and the British government was not the neutral arbiter that many Newfoundlanders thought it should have been. Yet there was a democratic vote by secret ballot, while none of the other provinces in Canada had a referendum on whether to join Canada. Confederation in 1867 was a deal worked out by political elites and voters did not get to decide. Not only did Newfoundlanders and Labradorians have a vote, but the presentation of proposed terms of union in the nightly broadcasts of the Convention presented a clear idea of the issues.

Smallwood and the Drive to "Modernize"

On the date of union, the federal government appointed Smallwood to form an interim government until the first provincial election could be held. He quickly established a provincial branch of the Liberal Party of Canada— also the majority party in the Canadian Parliament—with himself as leader. Smallwood's anti-confederate opponents, as a result, became Progressive

A CBC Radio drama by the London Theatre Company, directed by Paul O'Neill (seated). From left: John Holmes, Dawn Lesley, Charles Mardel, Norman Welch, Valerie Hermanni, Ruth Perkins, David Ryder, and Avis Lennard.

Conservatives. As premier, Smallwood had many advantages in election campaigns. Federal government transfers to individuals, such as family allowances and old age pensions, were now extended to Newfoundlanders and Labradorians, and Smallwood took personal credit for the cash flowing into many households. Most candidates running for the Conservatives had opposed confederation, and seemed to be fighting a battle they had already lost. The victorious Liberals dominated island constituencies outside the Avalon Peninsula and in Labrador.

Smallwood saw the sea as the source of Newfoundland's backwardness and put much of his attention into industrial developments. He strove to industrialize Newfoundland through a number of initiatives that his critics characterized as "develop or perish." His Liberal government used the accumulated surplus of the preceding Commission to entice foreign businessmen to found a number of industries. Making use of the connections of the Latvian-born Director of Economic Development, Alfred Valdmanis, the government enlisted the help of a number of German industrialists to open factories in the 1950s. One or two companies, such as North Star Cement in Corner Brook, thrived, but some of the entrepreneurs had taken the money from the financially naive Smallwood without intending to create the promised industry. Others had honest intentions, but upon arriving in Newfoundland found that business opportunities were not as rosy as Smallwood had represented them. Though backed by the provincial government, there were few successes and Valdmanis later pleaded guilty to having solicited bribes from would-be investors. The failures and corruption did much to diminish Smallwood's reputation. This was followed by larger projects that Smallwood hoped would kick-start industrial development. But his government's support for a third pulp and paper mill in Stephenville, and an oil refinery in Come By Chance, for example, resulted in large costs to taxpayers and disappointing results.

The first provincial government wanted to create a modern, educated workforce for the industries it promoted, and, in the quarter-century following confederation, hundreds of schools were built throughout the province, including long-overdue regional high schools. Compulsory education had been introduced in Newfoundland in 1942 and the expansion in availability of schools after 1949, combined with an improved economy and the benefits of family allowances, made at least a basic education possible for children of all classes and regions. Curriculum, the hiring of teachers, and other general education policies for the publicly funded school system remained under the control of denominational school boards, though rationalization and the 1969 amalgamation of the major Protestant boards did lessen the numbers of school boards from some 300 in the mid-1960s to thirty-five within ten years. The government offered financial incentives to encourage teachers to improve their qualifications.

Smallwood's government also built a system of vocational colleges in the province and raised the status of Memorial College to a degree-granting institution in 1949. As well as educating the young teachers needed for the rapidly expanding school system, the university was to be the centre for study of the province's history, culture, and economy. Within ten years it had outgrown the Parade Street campus and in 1961 moved north to Elizabeth Avenue. By the end of the decade the university had added a nursing and medical school and offered doctorate programmes in several fields. In 1975 it opened a two-year affiliated college at Corner Brook, soon named Sir Wilfred Grenfell College, which later expanded its original arts and science curriculum and offered students new options such as its highly respected fine arts programme. Memorial University played a central role in the social and cultural changes of the province. Several generations of teachers trained at Memorial staffed schools throughout the island and Labrador. Professional accountants, engineers, and skilled tradespeople who had been educated at Memorial and the other local post-secondary facilities could be found in nearly every activity.

In addition to educational improvements, the Liberal government also invested in other infrastructure—roads, hospitals, and electrification, for example—that would modernize the province. This was badly needed, and improved the quality of people's lives. However, in order to provide adequate services to everyone at a reasonable cost, the government implemented controversial resettlement programmes. Small rural communities had been disappearing since at least the start of the twentieth century, everywhere in the western world, not just in Newfoundland. Yet Newfoundland and Labrador continued to have a large number of dispersed settlements which were expensive to serve with the modern standards of health and education that people expected. By subsidizing moving costs, the government accelerated the existing trend, saving money in the long run. On occasion the government was heavy-handed toward communities it wanted to resettle, taking away services to force people to choose to move to larger "growth centres." Smallwood hoped that these new urban communities would have large enough populations to provide an industrial workforce, and become sites of a Newfoundland industrial revolution. Unfortunately, too few jobs materialized outside of the resource extraction industries of logging, mining, and the fishery, and the sons and daughters of many of those who had been resettled felt a great sense of loss that they had not been given the choice to live in their grandparents' homes.

While the forestry and fishery remained the largest industries, these too were mechanizing and now fewer workers were needed. Chain saws in the woods, offshore trawlers and fish plants that produced frozen fish, rather than the salted cod which had been Newfoundland's staple export for centuries, seemed modern and progressive, but mechanization meant that these industries did not provide enough year-round work to sustain many families. Moreover, these industries were unable to absorb the growing numbers of workers now that the baby boomers were entering the labour force. Mining communities did much better at providing year-round good wages, but inevitably the ore bodies were depleted and the companies left. The federal government filled some of the gaps in incomes by extending social payments such as unemployment insurance to fishermen. But in the long run, the highly capitalized fishing, mining, and logging industries took too large a portion of the natural resources to be permanently self-sustaining.

Workers organized to respond to these problems in the resource industries, sometimes resulting in bitter disputes such as the 1959 International Woodworkers of America (IWA) strike in central Newfoundland. The paper companies had maintained high wages among those who worked in the mills, but kept labour costs in the woods low by hiring sub-contractors to provide the wood. These sub-contractors had to underbid each other to win the contract and their profit then depended upon paying low wages to the loggers. The IWA took up the plight of loggers, who lived with low pay and poor working conditions. While earlier in his life Smallwood had flirted with socialism, this strike prompted him to side with capital rather than labour. He condemned the IWA as communists and gangsters, while the death of a police officer on the picket line gave him the excuse to outlaw the union.

Members of the CODCO theatrical troupe. From left: Mary Walsh, Diane Olsen, Cathy Jones, Robert Joy, Tommy Sexton, Greg Malone, and Andy Jones (photo: P. Hall, courtesy of Archives and Manuscripts, Memorial University Library).

This revealed that Smallwood was not the friend to the working man he had pretended to be.

Industrialization had not been an unqualified benefit. It had ecological costs. For example, immense areas in Labrador and on the island had been flooded to create reservoirs for hydro-electric generating stations. It also had great human costs. Miners at the St. Lawrence fluorspar mine suffered debilitating effects from exposure to dust and radon gas; workers on offshore fishing vessels faced more immediate risks to life and limb. These changes were accompanied by a revitalized place for trade unions. By the 1970s the Newfoundland Fishermen Food and Allied Workers Union (NFFAWU), for example, had organized both those who fished in trawlers and worked in fish plants, and collectively negotiated better prices, wages, and safety standards.

The generation that grew up as Canadians had aspirations that their grandfathers rarely entertained, but there was a reaction to the drive to modernize. Since the Conservatives in the House of Assembly were ineffectual and Smallwood effectively muzzled dissent within the Liberal party, the press and the university community became the only effective opposition. Former Smallwood ally Harold Horwood attacked Smallwood's development strategy in the *Evening Telegram*. While faculty at Memorial criticized such heavy-handed programmes of social engineering as the resettlement policies, many students turned to the Progressive Conservative Party in hope that it could provide a generational change in provincial leadership.

Upper Churchill Falls in Labrador (photo: William Rompkey).

Commentators and artists, who worked outside either the political process or the university, combined dissatisfaction with the way the province was changing with a renewed nationalism. Some urban people felt they had lost something essential to their culture and tried to recover it. Former provincial cabinet minister Ted Russell created a nostalgic radio series, *Tales from Pigeon Inlet*, which portrayed a vibrant outport community that contrasted with the Smallwood rhetoric that everything in the past was poor and that confederation was the gateway to "the happy province." Similarly, Ray Guy's satirical newspaper columns appealed to Newfoundlanders and Labradorians to remember their distinctive traditions and identity. His columns also made Smallwood a figure of fun rather than someone to be feared, and helped galvanize a new generation of politicians to challenge Smallwood's hegemony over government.

Guy's jibes appealed to young people who came of age after the Confederation debate. Many creative people, such as the actors in CODCO and the Mummers Troupe, criticized the unquestioning embrace of American popular culture and the development policies of the government. The musicians of Figgy Duff, for example, scoured the outports to collect folk music which they arranged for electric instruments to make it relevant to a new generation. These artists created a self-consciously nationalistic Newfoundland popular culture. By the end of the century several Newfoundland novelists had engaged with the history and contemporary life of the country and earned international success. Nationalism would wax and wane over the next few decades, but the legacy of a confident Newfoundland artistic community remained.

Specific groups also experienced a reawakening during the 1970s. Newfoundlanders of French heritage, benefiting from Canadian government policies of bilingualism, formed several groups to preserve and enhance the French language and culture within the province. Varied groups within Labrador also found common cause in their resentment of the way that people on the island of Newfoundland exploited the resources but paid little attention to the aspirations of the Labrador people. Efforts to form a New Labrador Party had brief success, but such ideas as the creation of a Labrador flag had a longer lasting effect in cementing a feeling of Labrador identity.

Unlike some of his critics, Smallwood's vision of a strong prosperous Newfoundland continued to be based upon large scale economic development. He used government money to support several megaprojects which he hoped would promote economic development. International investors built a paper mill at Stephenville, an oil refinery at Come By Chance, and a massive hydroelectric generating station at Churchill Falls in Labrador. Each of these was a mixed success. The paper mill had a chequered financial history and the oil refinery went bankrupt and was closed for many years before reopening in 1987. Churchill Falls made a great deal of money for the Québec-owned utility, Hydro-Québec, but under the terms of a long-term sales agreement returned little to Newfoundland. Each of these deals, especially the last, became symbolic of Newfoundland's experience of having entered into unfair deals with foreign capitalists who got the benefit of Newfoundland resources while the Newfoundland taxpayer bore the costs.

The desire of younger citizens to lessen the influence of patronage and nepotism and to make government more open, democratic, and professional became difficult to resist. Smallwood attempted to revitalize his party by bringing younger men with considerable talent into the cabinet. But he was unable to relinquish power, and few of these people remained in the cabinet, and under Smallwood's control, for long. Smallwood announced his retirement in 1969, but he could not imagine any man or woman filling his shoes, particularly the front-runner, John Crosbie. Smallwood therefore ran for the leadership, and a remarkably bitter contest pitted the younger generation, which supported Crosbie, against an older generation of Smallwood loyalists. Although Smallwood won on the convention floor, many Liberals defected to the Conservatives rather than remain in his party.

Sensing that Smallwood was vulnerable, Frank Moores left his seat as a Member of Parliament to lead the PCs. The October 1971 election resulted in a tie, with the balance of power held by an independent member elected in Labrador. Rather than concede defeat, Smallwood held on to the premiership without calling the legislature into session so that he had time to convince some opposition members to join him. Comical political skulduggery ensued as both parties tried to induce members of the House of Assembly to switch political allegiance. Smallwood finally resigned, and Moores called an election. The Progressive Conservatives won a majority of seats in 1972; Moores, however, had the bad fortune to be premier as several of the megaprojects failed. On the positive side, he reintroduced democracy to the cabinet and some of the talented people in his government made much needed legislative reforms. One cabinet minister in particular, Brian Peckford, exemplified a nationalistic agenda which held out the hope that Newfoundland could get control over its natural resources and leverage that into prosperity by demanding royalties. The discovery of oil off the island's coast gave Newfoundlanders and Labradorians hope that oil wealth could allow the province to reduce its dependence upon federal transfer payments.

The Costs of Modernization

A quarter of a century after confederation Newfoundland was a significantly different society than it had been in 1949. The late 1960s was a time of cultural and political struggle throughout the western world, and Newfoundlanders also debated public policy, women's place in society, and other social changes. The influence of the churches was diminished as society became more secular. Effective antibiotics had finally ended the devastating effects of tuberculosis, which had indeed been a "white plague" for generations of Newfoundlanders and Labradorians. Increased access to effective birth control, longer education, and rising economic expectations saw young Newfoundland and Labrador couples join the national trend to have smaller families. At the time of confederation Newfoundland had the highest birth rate in the country but in the 1960s this declined sharply to parallel national trends. By the late 1990s, in a remarkable demographic change, the province had the lowest birth rates in the country. Reflecting the continued and rising emigration of young people, this decrease signalled major social and economic problems for the province, particularly for rural areas.

The rural way of life also seemed to be under attack by animal rights activists. In the twentieth century, the seal hunt remained important in the household economy in some areas, but retained only a fraction of the economic importance it had during the nineteenth. By the 1970s publicity-seeking activists outside Newfoundland seized upon the admittedly gruesome images of the killing of seals, pressuring the Government of Canada into regulating how the animals were to be harvested. Hollywood celebrities seemed to be threatening an important part of Newfoundlanders' heritage and culture. Although seals were not a threatened species, image won over substance and the hunt for young harp seals was banned in 1987. The landsman

The Hibernia oil production platform with a supply vessel, on the Grand Banks of Newfoundland (courtesy of Hibernia Management and Development Company Ltd.).

hunt of mature seals continued—a last remnant of the once-important industry which had been key to the settlement and development of Newfoundland and Labrador.

As demographic and economic changes forced Newfoundlanders to seek new paths forward, women insisted on a greater voice in shaping their province's future. The federal Royal Commission on the Status of Women, which reported in 1970, rejuvenated the women's movement. Newfoundland women made six submissions to the Commission, most of which focused on work-related issues such as pay equity, child care, and discrimination against married women workers. Throughout the 1970s women all over the province formed local Status of Women's Councils and other groups to follow up on the Commission's 166 recommendations. This second wave of women's activism saw women form groups at the grassroots level, led by local rural and urban women of various economic and educational backgrounds, sexual orientation, and ethnicity. Native women met in Nain in 1978 to discuss their concerns, including family violence, alcohol abuse, limited child care for working mothers, and loss of culture and language. They went on to form smaller local self-support and lobbying groups to address these and other issues. While these organizations shared some concerns such as the limited presence of women in political life and threats to women's health and safety, they varied in their priorities and methods. Despite varied, and at times conflicting, visions of feminism, the modern women's movement has had some notable successes, such as the 1979 Matrimonial Property Act which legislated equal division of marital assets after divorce or separation.

Native people, too, demanded control over their own destiny after centuries of having outsiders make decisions for them. In the 1950s, clergy and government officials had sometimes gone as far as relocating communities without consultation, leaving Natives in areas in which they could be administered effectively but where the land could not support them. Responding in part to a North American wide resurgence of Native activism and in part to the challenges faced by their communities, Natives created new organizations to pursue their agenda. By the 1970s Natives began to negotiate land claims, moved toward self-government, and tried to reinvigorate their culture. For decades the school system had discouraged native languages at the same time that economic changes eroded Native people's economy without replacing it with a sound alternative. Natives would no longer be ignored when economic developments affected them. The Inuit of Labrador, for example, signed a comprehensive land agreement and in 2006 elected their own government in the new territory of Nunatsiavut.

During the 1980s, the new government of Brian Peckford capitalized on frustration with Ottawa and a general feeling among Newfoundlanders that they had to get a fair share of the value of their resources. He won a series of elections by skilfully presenting a vote for him as a vote to end resource giveaways, and by demanding a fairer deal within confederation. The combative politics made for good electioneering, but the provincial government continued to run deficits and earned few concessions from Ottawa. That did not prevent Peckford from signing a "roads for rails" deal by which the federal government closed the railway, so long a symbol of Newfoundland's effort to industrialize, in exchange for money to improve the highway system.

While one generation's symbolic industry, the railway, became an object of nostalgia, people placed their hope for a better tomorrow in offshore oil and gas. Unfortunately from the province's perspective, the federal government claimed it owned the resources of the continental shelf—a claim upheld by the Supreme Court of Canada. Joint provincial and federal management of offshore oil and gas was gained only when a Progressive Conservative minority government was elected in Ottawa. The risks of industrialization were made concrete in 1982 when the oil exploration rig, the *Ocean Ranger*, capsized in a storm and all eighty-four crew members died. This reminder of the harsh environment offshore did not prevent oil companies from developing several oil fields, each of which became a significant source of revenue for the provincial government by the 1990s. While government finances improved and the industry provided many high wage jobs, the economic growth did not extend much beyond the St. John's area. Rural areas continued to experience high levels of unemployment and a rapid decline in population.

While people waited for the promised oil wealth, rural families increasingly saw their children leave for the prospect of a better life in other provinces. In 1989 the new Liberal leader, Clyde Wells, benefited from the electorate's desire for a more business-like government. Voters expected the cool-headed Wells to have a better relationship with Ottawa, but that did not happen. He remained committed to his vision of a centralized federal union and rescinded Newfoundland's approval of the Meech Lake Constitutional Accord. Although this earned him regard in some circles as a man of principle, it also brought him the enmity of the federal government. He cut government expenditure in an effort to balance the budget, which had run deficits since 1949, creating civil service labour discontent, and his unpopular and ultimately unsuccessful effort to sell the crown corporation Newfoundland Hydro dissipated much of the goodwill he had built up.

Wells was premier through one of the most difficult times in the province's post-confederation history. Beginning in 1989, allegations emerged about the sexual abuse of children by Roman Catholic priests in several parishes throughout the province. This was followed by reports that some Christian Brothers in charge of Mount Cashel Orphanage, an almost-century-old Catholic institution, had abused their charges for decades. A subsequent public enquiry confirmed the allegations and exposed disturbing evidence of cover-ups and mishandling which shook people's faith in both their religious leaders and their legal system.

The abuse scandals made it impossible for the church to claim the high moral ground in its dispute with the government over ending publicly funded denominational schools. Opinion polls indicated growing public support for integrating schools, especially as the declining number of school-age children made the financial waste of duplication of facilities and administrators more apparent. After two supportive referenda and a constitutional amendment, Wells's successor, Brian Tobin, ended the 155-year-old denominational education system in 1998. Tobin, who had a been a Member of Parliament before moving to St. John's to take over the premiership, also brought an improved relationship with Ottawa.

Federal-provincial relations were important, not the least because the Government of Canada had jurisdiction over the fishery. The extension of Canadian fisheries jurisdiction to 200 miles offshore in 1977 had raised the possibility that better management of the fish stocks would ensure a bright future. Unfortunately fish science was imprecise, and quotas were as much a product of political negotiation as they were measurements of the size of the fish stock and the amount which could be harvested. For many years during the 1970s and 1980s it was not apparent that the number of cod in the sea was less than thought, a fact which was in part hidden by new technologies which were effective in catching more of the dwindling resource. By 1992 the situation had reached a crisis point. The federal government imposed a moratorium upon harvesting cod in what had been hitherto the most productive area—the northern cod stocks. To lessen the social effect, compensation was paid to many families, and others of those who had fished switched to the snow crab. Unfortunately, the diminished cod population did not rebound once it was no longer being fished—environmental factors and the continued taking of some cod meant that the moratorium did not result in a halt in the decline of the number of fish. For all that, the economic loss devastated many communities and families, but the moratorium was also symbolic of the end of a way of life that had defined Newfoundland for nearly 500 years. The near extinction of the northern cod, which had been the country's staple export, had a cultural effect felt even by Newfoundlanders and Labradorians who had themselves never fished.

A century after the settling of the French Shore dispute and the completion of the trans-island railway, historians are able to reflect on the successes and failures of Newfoundland and Labrador's twentieth-century effort to modernize. The society had become more secular; the influence of clergy and the separation of people into sectarian groups in schools and other social institutions had declined. The government's desire to industrialize and make the province like the more developed parts of North America was a mixed success. But Newfoundlanders had become modern. As the country became more urban, family activities such as growing food and cutting firewood diminished. Most Newfoundlanders and Labradorians now live in towns and cities and work for wages rather than bartering the products of their labour for life's necessities. They share North American tastes for consumer goods, reliance on modern technology such as the Internet, and expectations of government services. Newfoundlanders and Labradorians, nonetheless, retain a unique culture and sense of identity, based partly on a deep interest in, and connection to, their own past.

Time Line

1915	James P. Howley publishes *The Beothucks, or Red Indians.*
1916	1 July: Newfoundland Regiment decimated at Beaumont Hamel.
1918	Conscription introduced; First World War ends; Spanish flu arrives in Newfoundland.
1919	John Alcock and Arthur Whitten Brown make the first nonstop transatlantic flight from St. John's; Spanish flu epidemic hits Labrador.
1923	Government takes over the railway and coastal steam service.
1925	Corner Brook pulp and paper mill begins production; legislature passes the Women's Suffrage Bill; Memorial University College opens.
1927	Privy Council defines the Labrador boundary in Newfoundland's favour; Gerald S. Doyle publishes *The Old Time Songs and Poetry of Newfoundland.*
1928	Buchans mine opens.
1929	Burin peninsula tsunami.
1932	Riot outside the Colonial Building.
1933	Royal Commission chaired by Lord Amulree examines condition of Newfoundland; Elisabeth Greenleaf publishes *Ballads and Sea Songs of Newfoundland.*
1934	Responsible government suspended; Commission of Government installed; Maud Karpeles publishes *Folk Songs from Newfoundland.*
1936	Margaret Duley publishes *The Eyes of the Gull.*
1937	J.R. Smallwood publishes *The Book of Newfoundland.*
1938	Gander Airport opens.
1939	Broadcasting Corporation of Newfoundland formed.
1940	Leased bases deal between Britain and the United States.
1941	Arrival of *Edmund B. Alexander*, troop ship; construction of Goose Bay air base, Labrador.

1942	German submarines sink ore carriers off Bell Island and the SS *Caribou* in the Gulf of St. Lawrence.
1946	Election of the National Convention.
1948	Confederation wins the second referendum; negotiation of terms of union with Canada.
1949	Newfoundland with Labrador becomes a Canadian province (31 March); J.R. Smallwood, premier of a Liberal provincial government; Memorial University College becomes Memorial University of Newfoundland.
1953	Start of the government-sponsored resettlement programme.
1955	First television service, CJON, opens.
1959	IWA strike in central Newfoundland; relocation of Inuit from Hebron; David Blackwood begins The Lost Party, a series of prints of the Newfoundland disaster.
1962	Mining begins at Labrador City.
1965	Trans Canada Highway across Newfoundland completed; first solo exhibit of work of artist Christopher Pratt.
1966	Bell Island iron mines close; agreement reached on development of Churchill Falls.
1967	Bay d'Espoir hydro development on-stream.
1969	Medicare instituted; passenger rail service closed.
1970	Formation of Fishermen's Union (NFFAW); Percy Janes publishes *House of Hate*.
1972	Frank Moores heads the first PC provincial government; first power from Churchill Falls is delivered to Hydro-Québec; Cassie Brown publishes *Death on the Ice*.
1973	Come By Chance refinery opens; Stephenville mill opens; first performance by CODCO theatre troupe.
1975	Cable television comes to Newfoundland; Sir Wilfred Grenfell College opens.

1976	Come By Chance refinery closes: bankruptcy.
1977	Linerboard mill in Stephenville closes; fluorspar mines at St. Lawrence close; 200-nautical-mile jurisdiction over offshore resources established; Brigitte Bardot protests the seal hunt.
1978	Norse site at L'Anse aux Meadows is declared a UNESCO World Heritage Site.
1979	Offshore oil discoveries confirmed; first women appointed to a provincial cabinet: Hazel Newhook and Lynn Verge.
1980	New provincial flag is adopted; Newfoundland and Labrador Arts Council established; Figgy Duff releases self-titled album.
1982	Loss of *Ocean Ranger*; Europe bans import of seal pup pelts; *Dictionary of Newfoundland English* is published.
1983	Construction of the Trans-Labrador Highway begins; Mi'kmaq of Conne River recognized as status Indians.
1984	Supreme Court of Canada rules that the Hibernia oil field belongs to Canada; formation of Fishery Products International.
1985	Signature of the Atlantic Accord; Buchans mine closes.
1986	Official end to the killing of seal pups or "whitecoats."
1988	Labrador becomes a separate federal riding; federal-provincial agreement to close the Railway in return for $800 million for roads.
1990	Agreement on Hibernia oil field development.
1992	Cod moratorium imposed.
1994	US military base at Argentia closed.
1995	Discovery of Voisey's Bay mineral deposit.
1996	Agreement on Terra Nova oil field development.
1997	John Cabot 500th-anniversary celebrations; referendum approves end of denominational school system.

EPILOGUE

James K. Hiller

In 2002, the provincial government established a royal commission to investigate "Renewing and Strengthening Our Place in Canada." Its report disappeared from the public agenda soon after it appeared in 2003 (along with the government which appointed it) possibly because it was long on generalities and short on practical recommendations. Nevertheless, the fact that such a royal commission was appointed reflects current discussion and ideas about the position of Newfoundland and Labrador in the twenty-first century.

There is a profound and pervasive sense of disappointment that confederation with Canada has failed to make the province prosperous and respected, in spite of its natural and human resources. Indeed, as the province's population declines and ages, there is justifiable uncertainty about the future. At the same time, there exists a local nationalism which articulates a deep attachment to the province, expressed most obviously in the arts and heritage sectors—in literature, music, the visual arts, museums, building preservation, and archives.

This mingling of pride and pessimism affects historians as much as anyone else. History, after all, is not static. There will never be a single, authoritative, and final history of Newfoundland and Labrador because the writing of history is an ongoing dialogue in which the changing perspectives of the present continually modify our views of the past. Moreover, individual historians have their own idiosyncrasies, and researchers will always continue to find new evidence. Judge Prowse might have been the final word in 1895, but not today.

The chapters in this short book do not, therefore, constitute a final interpretation of this province's history. They summarize the enormous amount of historical research that has been carried out in the past forty years through the perspective of each author. However, the book also reflects a conviction that Newfoundland and Labrador has a significant and distinct history which deserves to be much better known, not only within the province, but across Canada.

The importance of this country and its fisheries in the early modern North Atlantic world—a place once fought over—is attracting increasing attention, as is the later emergence of unique identities and cultures, both Aboriginal and European. Its role in the world wars of the twentieth century is also a subject of revived interest. But at the same time we have to ask why the country has been plagued by out-migration since the eighteenth century; why responsible government ended in near-bankruptcy; and why the optimism of the 1950s has disappeared. There is also the question of a small country's difficult and sometimes confrontational relationship with a distant imperial centre—once London, now Ottawa.

Newfoundlanders and Labradorians thus have to face their past in a clear, balanced, and informed way. The royal commission's historical summary is a good example of this approach. Myths, legends, and stories may fuel the tourist industry, but they have little to do with a future which, it seems, will be increasingly dependent on a hard-headed assessment of Newfoundland and Labrador's past experience and its current potential.

This book will have served its purpose if it informs debate about such issues, and if it reminds Newfoundlanders, Labradorians, and Canadians, in general, that the province is a special place with a stubborn local nationalism that has deep historical roots. Canada, it might be argued, began here.

GLOSSARY

Readers may also refer to the Newfoundland and Labrador Heritage Website Glossary at www.heritage.nf.ca/glossary.html

Bank fishery: fishery centred on the great fishing banks of the Grand Banks, off Newfoundland, carried out by fleets who came from New England, Nova Scotia, Lower Canada, France, Spain, Portugal, Italy, the West Country of England, and, by the nineteenth century, Newfoundland. The bank fishery flourished from the seventeenth to the twentieth century.

Bye-boat: an open boat kept in Newfoundland, and used in the inshore fishery during the summer by a migratory bye-boat keeper.

Court of Oyer and Terminer: literally, a court to hear and determine. This court could deal with all crimes except treason, which had to be heard in a British Court.

Dry fish: lightly salted, air-dried cod.

English Shore: the east coast from Trepassey to Bonavista Bay, after 1565 seasonally frequented by West Country fishing crews and settled by fisher folk after 1610.

Fishermen's Protective Union: a powerful fishers' union formed in 1908 with a mandate for collective action. The founding president was William Coaker. The FPU faded out of existence by 1960.

Fishing admiral: the fishing master arriving first in a particular harbour in spring. He could claim first choice of fishing rooms and the right to enforce the traditional custom of the fishery during the ensuing fishing season. Though called "admirals," fishing admirals were not naval officers.

Fishing room: the land on a shore from which resident planters or migratory ship fishermen prosecuted the inshore fishery. Also called a plantation.

Fishing ship: a ship coming to Newfoundland for the summer, carrying fishermen and provisions for an inshore fishery, which would be prosecuted from open boats. (Before 1713 the English at Newfoundland did not fish from the ship itself but from small open boats.) These so-called fishing ships also often carried fish to market.

Flake: a scaffold of poles, supporting a rough surface of evergreen boughs, used to dry salt cod.

Floater fishery, *see* **Migratory fishery.**

Floaters: fishers at Labrador who moved around during the season in their schooners, rather than fishing from a fixed location.

FPU: *see* **Fishermen's Protective Union**.

Freight, to: to hire the services of a ship and its crew.

French Shore: in the Treaty of Utrecht (1713) France recognized British sovereignty over the island of Newfoundland, but retained the right to fish in season on the coast between Cape Bonavista and Pointe Riche. The limits were changed in 1783 to Cape St. John to Cape Ray. France gave up the fishery in 1904.

Governor: 1. Naval governor. A British naval officer with a professional posting as colonial administrator, e.g., in Newfoundland, governors George Clinton, 1732-1741, and Francis Pickmore, 1816-1818. The naval governor was also commodore of the naval squadron at Newfoundland. **2. Civil governor**. A non-military colonial administrator. The civil governorship was a political appointment falling under the purview of the Colonial Office in England. Newfoundland's first civil governor was Thomas Cochrane, 1825-1834, appointed after Newfoundland achieved colonial status in 1825.

Green fish: synonym for wet fish, heavily salted in brine.

Green man: a novice or "youngster" in the fishery.

Labrador fishery: the Labrador fishery was carried out by Newfoundlanders who migrated to Labrador from summer to autumn. Fishers were either Stationers, who stayed on the land and fished the nearby coast; or Floaters, who stayed on their schooners and fished various fishing grounds. The Floater fishery was also known as the Schooner fishery. Fishers from Conception Bay were the largest group engaged in the Labrador fishery.

Migratory fishery: **1.** the practice of migrating to Newfoundland during the fishing season and returning home to continental Europe or Britain afterwards; or **2.** the practice of migrating to Labrador during the fishing season and returning back home to Newfoundland afterwards.

Moravian Church: also known as the Unitas Fratrum or the Brethren, the Moravians were a Protestant Episcopal church that traced its origins back to sixteenth-century Europe. In the eighteenth century it experienced a renewal as well as a new dedication to overseas missionary service, including Greenland and eventually Labrador. Moravians made their first journey to Labrador in 1752.

Newfoundland Patriotic Association: the voluntary organization responsible for all aspects of Newfoundland's war effort between 1914 and 1917, when its duties were taken over by a newly created Department of Militia. The NPA's activity in the Second World War was limited to fundraising.

Newfoundlander: someone born in Newfoundland. This term was first attested with this meaning in 1765.

NPA: *see* **Newfoundland Patriotic Association.**

Nursery for seamen: an assumption, dating to the sixteenth century, that the fishery served as a work place where landsmen acquired skills and experience that transformed them into capable sailors who might then be available for service in the navies of their homelands in time of war.

Passengers: persons other than a ship's crew carried between the British Isles and Newfoundland. Passengers might be bye-boat-men, planters, or their servants.

Petit Nord: the French term for the east coast of Newfoundland's Great Northern Peninsula, including the Baie Verte Peninsula, where Bretons and Normans prosecuted a migratory inshore fishery from the sixteenth century until 1904.

Plantation: the waterfront property from which a Newfoundland planter prosecuted the fishery.

Planter: a resident of Newfoundland who owned property, normally a fishing plantation or room.

Prime Minister: head of state, used in the Newfoundland context for head of state during the later years of responsible government era. From 1832 to 1909 the term "Premier" was used, while Prime Minister became the norm from 1909 to 1934.

Proprietary colony: one of the early colonies owned outright by a proprietor, e.g., the seventeenth-century colonies at Ferryland and Cupids.

Prosecution (of a fishery): the ongoing work at the fishery; engagement in the fishing industry.

Quintal: 112 pounds (50.8 kg.), a traditional unit of weight for salt fish (pronounced and sometimes spelled "kental").

Refuse cod: dried and salted codfish at the bottom level of the standard grades for processed codfish.

Representative government: a form of colonial government in British North America. Under representative government, the legislature consisted of an elected House of Assembly and an appointed Legislative Council. Most legislative Councillors were also members, with the Governor, of the Executive Council, which was the colony's government. In Newfoundland, representative government lasted from 1832 to 1855.

Responsible government: introduced in most British colonies of settlement in the mid-nineteenth century, the system of responsible government gave control of all domestic affairs, including financial matters, to the colonial government. The imperial government retained responsibility for imperial and external affairs. The government, headed by a premier (prime minister after 1909), was formed by the political party holding the majority of seats in the House of Assembly. Newfoundland had responsible government from 1855 to 1933.

Sack ship: a ship coming to Newfoundland to buy a cargo of fish to carry to market and sometimes, loosely, any ship carrying fish to market or any cargo ship.

Schooner fishery: *see* **Labrador fishery**.

Servant: within the fishery, a person employed and receiving a wage.

Ship fishermen: fishers arriving in Newfoundland on so-called fishing ships to prosecute an inshore fishery in boats.

Society for the Propagation of the Gospel: established in 1703, the SPG was the missionary arm of the Church of England in Great Britain's overseas colonies and territories.

St. Peter's: name of St. Pierre during British ownership.

Stage: a rough wooden wharf with an enclosed space on top, used for unloading and processing fish.

Stationer fishery: *see* **Labrador fishery**.

Stationer: fishers at Labrador who worked from one particular cove or harbour.

Surrogate: one appointed to act as judge in the vice-admiralty court in place of a regular judge; a deputy or substitute. In the late 1700s and early 1800s, the governor could appoint naval officers and certain others to act as his substitute to help administer fishery regulations and other laws in Newfoundland and

Labrador. Their courts were called Surrogate Courts.

Tierce: unit of measure for a wooden cask larger than a barrel but smaller than a hogshead. In liquid measure, a third of a pipe (i.e., 35 imperial gallons, 42 wine gallons, or approximately 133 litres). The term tierce was commonly used for export in the salmon fishery and equalled 300 pounds or approximately 135 kilograms.

Train oil: cod liver oil, whale oil, or seal oil shipped to Europe in barrels for industrial use, as lubricant or fuel.

Train vat: a large wooden container used to collect train oil.

Truck system: a system of payments in kind by which merchants advanced provisions to nominally independent households, on credit, against their expected catch of fish.

West Country: traditionally, the English counties of Somerset, Dorset, Devon, and Cornwall, but in Newfoundland and Labrador history the emphasis is on Devon and Dorset, which were most heavily involved in the Newfoundland trade.

Western Adventurers: English investors in the West Country migratory fishery at Newfoundland in the first part of the seventeenth century, e.g., the White and Taverner families of Trinity.

Wet fish: cod heavily salted in brine.

Winterhousing: seasonal residence inland, close to supplies of firewood.

Women's Patriotic Association: an island-wide association formed at the beginning of the First World War to help soldiers in their work defending the British Empire. The WPA sent them money, knitted items and comforts such as tobacco, and prepared medical supplies for the Red Cross, which organization it also helped during the Second World War. The WPA was also interested in the welfare of families at home and contributed towards health care, child care, education through scholarships, and women's suffrage. It disbanded shortly after the war ended but was re-formed for similar purposes during the Second World War.

WPA: *see* **Women's Patriotic Association**.

Youngster: a novice in the fishery; also "green man."

SUGGESTED READING

General Reference

Mel Baker's Home Page: www.ucs.mun.ca/~melbaker/

Centre for Newfoundland Studies: www.library.mun.ca/qeii/cns/index.php

Dictionary of Canadian Biography (Toronto: University of Toronto Press, 1966-: www.biographi.ca/index2.html)

Encyclopedia of Newfoundland and Labrador.

Hans Rollmann's Website: www.ucs.mun.ca/~hrollman/

Harris, R.C. (ed.) and G. Matthews (cartographer/designer). *The Historical Atlas of Canada, vol. 1: From the Beginning to 1800* (Toronto: University of Toronto Press, 1988).

Janzen, Olaf Uwe. "A Reader's Guide to the History of Newfoundland and Labrador to 1869" (Corner Brook: Sir Wilfred Grenfell College: www.swgc. mun.ca/nfld_history/index.htm)

Newfoundland and Labrador Heritage Website: www.heritage.nf.ca

Newfoundland and Labrador Studies: www.mun.ca/nls

Newfoundland Quarterly: www.newfoundlandquarterly.ca/

The Rooms, Museum Notes: www.therooms.ca/museum/mnotes1.asp

General Works

Cadigan, S. *Hope and Deception in Conception Bay. Merchant-Settler Relations in Newfoundland, 1785-1855* (Toronto: University of Toronto Press, 1995).

Fitzhugh, Lynne D. *The Labradorians. Voices from the Land of Cain* (St. John's: Breakwater Books, 1999).

Greene, J.P. *Between Damnation and Starvation. Priests and Merchants in Newfoundland Politics, 1745-1855* (Montreal: McGill-Queen's University Press, 1999).

Hiller, James K. and Peter Neary (eds.). *Newfoundland in the Nineteenth and Twentieth Centuries: Essays in Interpretation* (Toronto: University of Toronto Press, 1980).

Innis, H.A. *The Cod Fisheries* (Toronto: University of Toronto Press, 1954).

Kealey, L. (ed.). *Pursuing Equality: Historical Perspectives on Women in Newfoundland and Labrador* (St. John's: ISER, 1993).

McCann, Phillip. *Schooling in a Fishing Society: Education and Economic Conditions in Newfoundland and Labrador, 1836-1986* (St. John's: ISER, 1994).

Mannion, John (ed.). *The Peopling of Newfoundland: Essays in Historical Geography* (St. John's: ISER, 1977).

Matthews, Keith. "Historical Fence Building: A Critique of the Historiography of Newfoundland," *Newfoundland Studies,* 17/2 (2001), 143-65.

O'Flaherty, Patrick. *The Rock Observed: Studies in the Literature of Newfoundland* (Toronto: University of Toronto Press, 1979).

O'Flaherty, Patrick. *Old Newfoundland: A History to 1843* (St. John's: Long Beach Press, 1999).

O'Flaherty, Patrick. *Lost Country: The Rise and Fall of Newfoundland 1843-1933* (St. John's: Long Beach Press, 2005).

Rompkey, William. *The Story of Labrador* (Montreal: McGill-Queen's University Press, 2005).

Prehistory and Aboriginal Peoples

Brewster, Natalie. *The Inuit in Southern Labrador: The View from Snack Cove*, Occasional Papers in Northeastern Archaeology, 15 (St. John's: Copetown Press, 2006).

Etudes Inuit Studies, 4/1-2 (1980), Special Issue: The Inuit of Southern Quebec-Labrador.

Fitzhugh, William, Stephen Loring and Daniel Odess (eds.). *Honouring our Elders: A History of Eastern Arctic Archaeology, Contributions to Circumpolar Anthropology*, 2 (Washington, DC: The Smithsonian, 2002).

Ingstad, Helge and Anne Stine Ingstad. *The Viking Discovery of America: The Excavation of a Norse settlement in L'Anse aux Meadows, Newfoundland* (St. John's: Breakwater Books, 2000).

Lewis-Simpson, Shannon (ed.). *Vinland Revisited: The Norse World at the Turn of the First Millennium* (St. John's: Historic Sites Association, 2003).

Marshall, Ingeborg. *A History and Ethnography of the Beothuk* (Montreal: McGill-Queen's University Press, 1996).

Newfoundland Studies, 9/2 (1993), Special Issue: Archaeology in Newfoundland and Labrador.

Pastore, Ralph T. *Shanawdithit's People: The Archaeology of the Beothuks* (St. John's: Atlantic Archaeology, Ltd., 1992).

Renouf, M.A.P. *Ancient Culture Bountiful Seas: The Story of Port au Choix* (St. John's: Historic Sites Association, 1999).

Tuck, James A. *Ancient People of Port au Choix: The Excavation of an Archaic Indian Cemetery in Newfoundland*, Newfoundland Social and Economic Studies, 17 (St. John's: ISER, 1976).

Tuck, James A. *Newfoundland and Labrador Prehistory* (Toronto and New York: Van Nostrand, 1976).

Wallace, Birgitta. *Westward Vikings: The Saga of L'Anse aux Meadows* (St. John's: Historic Sites Association, 2006).

Early Modern Newfoundland and Labrador
(a) The Sixteenth and Seventeenth Centuries

Bulgin, Iona (ed.). *Cabot and His World Symposium: June 1997 Papers and Presentations* (St. John's: Newfoundland Historical Society, 1999).

Cell, Gillian T. (ed.). *Newfoundland Discovered, English Attempts at Colonization, 1610-1630* (London: Hakluyt Society, 1982).

Cell, Gillian T. *English Enterprise in Newfoundland, 1577-1660* (Toronto: University of Toronto Press, 1969).

Jones, Evan. "Alwyn Ruddock: 'John Cabot and the Discovery of America'," *Historical Research*, 80/208 (2007), 1-31.

Matthews, Keith (ed.). *Collection and Commentary on the Constitutional Laws of Seventeenth Century Newfoundland* (St. John's: Maritime History Group, Memorial University of Newfoundland, 1975).

Pope, Peter E. "Comparisons: Atlantic Canada," in Daniel Vickers (ed.), *A Companion to Colonial America* (Oxford: Blackwell, 2003), 489-507.

Pope, Peter E. "The English in Newfoundland in the Century after Cabot," *Avalon Chronicles*, 7 (2002), 1-22.

Pope, Peter E. *Fish Into Wine: The Newfoundland Plantation in the Seventeenth Century* (Chapel Hill, NC: University of North Carolina Press, 2004).

Pope, Peter E. *The Many Landfalls of John Cabot* (Toronto: University of Toronto Press, 1997).

Quinn, David B. *Sir Humphrey Gilbert and Newfoundland* (St. John's: Newfoundland Historical Society, 1983).

Williams, Alan F. *John Cabot and Newfoundland* (St. John's: Newfoundland Historical Society, 1996).

(b) The Eighteenth Century

Bannister, Jerry. *The Rule of the Admirals: Law, Custom, and Naval Government in Newfoundland, 1699-1832* (Toronto: University of Toronto Press, 2003).

Brière, Jean-François, "The French Fishery in the 18th Century," in James E. Candow and Carol Corbin (eds.), *How Deep Is The Ocean? Historical Essays on Canada's Atlantic Fishery* (Sydney, NS: University College of Cape Breton Press, 1997), 47-64.

Handcock, W. Gordon. *So longe as there comes noe women: Origins of English Settlement in Newfoundland* (St. John's: Breakwater Books, 1989).

Head, C. Grant. *Eighteenth Century Newfoundland: A Geographer's Perspective* (Toronto: McClelland & Stewart, 1976).

Nemec, Thomas F. "Trepassey, 1505-1840 A.D.: An Ethnohistorical Reconstruction of Anglo-Irish Outport Society," *The Newfoundland Quarterly*, 69/4 (March, 1973), 17-28.

Newfoundland Studies, 17/2 (Fall, 2001), Special Issue: The New Early Modern Newfoundland: The Eighteenth Century.

Rollmann, Hans. "Richard Edwards, John Campbell, and the Proclamation of Religious Liberty in Eighteenth-Century Newfoundland," *The Newfoundland Quarterly*, 80/2 (Fall 1984), 4-12.

Whiteley, William H. *James Cook in Newfoundland 1762-1767* (St. John's: Newfoundland Historical Society, 1975).

The Nineteenth and Twentieth Centuries

Alexander, David. *The Decay of Trade. An Economic History of the Newfoundland Saltfish Trade, 1935-1965* (St. John's: ISER, 1977).

Blake, Raymond. *Canadians at Last: Canada Integrates Newfoundland as a Province* (Toronto: University of Toronto Press, 1994, 2004).

Duley, Margot. *Where Once Our Mothers Stood We Stand. Women's Suffrage in Newfoundland, 1890-1925* (Charlottetown: Gynergy Press, 1993).

Fizzard, Garfield (ed.). *Amulree's Legacy: Truth Lies and Consequences* (St. John's: Newfoundland Historical Society, 2001).

Gwyn, Richard. *Smallwood, the Unlikely Revolutionary* (Toronto: McClelland and Stewart, 1968, 1972).

Hiller, James K. and Michael Harrington (eds.). *The Newfoundland National Convention, 1946-1948* (Montreal: McGill-Queen's University Press, 1995).

Hiller, James K. and Peter Neary (eds.). *Twentieth-Century Newfoundland: Explorations* (St. John's: Breakwater Books, 1993).

Hiller, James K. *Confederation: Deciding Newfoundland's Future 1934 to 1949* (St. John's: Newfoundland Historical Society, 1998).

Hiller, James. *The Newfoundland Railway, 1881-1949* (St. John's: Newfoundland Historical Society, 1981).

Jones, F. *Edward Feild, Bishop of Newfoundland, 1844-76* (St. John's: Newfoundland Historical Society, 1976).

MacKay, R.A. (ed.). *Newfoundland: Economic, Diplomatic and Strategic Studies* (Toronto: Oxford University Press, 1946).

MacKenzie, David. *Inside the Atlantic Triangle: Canada and the Entrance of Newfoundland into Confederation, 1939-1949* (Toronto: University of Toronto Press, 1986).

Martin, W. *Once Upon a Mine: The Story of Pre-Confederation Mines on the Island of Newfoundland* (Westmount, QC: Anlo, 1998).

McDonald, Ian. *"To Each His Own": William Coaker and the Fishermen's Protective Union in Newfoundland Politics, 1908-1925* (St. John's: ISER, 1987).

Neary, Peter. *Newfoundland in the North Atlantic World, 1929-1949* (Montreal: McGill-Queen's University Press, 1980).

Noel, S.J.R. *Politics in Newfoundland* (Toronto: University of Toronto Press, 1971).

Ryan, Shannon. *Fish Out of Water. The Newfoundland Saltfish Trade, 1814-1914* (St. John's: Breakwater Books, 1986).

Ryan, Shannon. *The Ice Hunters. A History of Newfoundland Sealing to 1914* (St. John's: Breakwater Books, 1994).

Thompson, F.F. *The French Shore Question in Newfoundland* (University of Toronto Press, 1961).

Wright, Miriam. *A Fishery for Modern Times: The State and the Industrialization of the Newfoundland Fishery, 1934-1968* (Don Mills, ON: Oxford University Press Canada, 2000).

Webb, Jeff A. *The Voice of Newfoundland: A Social History of the Broadcasting Corporation of Newfoundland, 1939-1949* (Toronto: University of Toronto Press, 2008).